WORLD
IN RECIPES

Michael Bateman

ROUND the WORLD IN RECIPES

Michael Bateman

British Library Cataloguing in Publication Data

Bateman, Michael
Round the World in Recipes
I. Title
641.5

ISBN 0 340 59155 2

First published 1993
Impression number 10 9 8 7 6 5 4 3 2 1
Year 1998 1997 1996 1995 1994 1993

Typeset by Wearset, Boldon, Tyne & Wear.
Printed in Great Britain for Hodder & Stoughton Educational, a division of Hodder Headline Plc, Mill Road, Dunton Green, Sevenoaks, Kent TN13 2YA by Cox and Wyman Ltd, Reading.

CONTENTS

Introduction

1 Vegetables and potatoes

Recipes

2 *Beans and pulses*

3 *Bread, pasta and pastry*

4 *Rice and grains*

5 *Fish, meat and dairy foods*

6 *Fruit salads and puddings*

ACKNOWLEDGEMENTS

I'm grateful to many dozens of colleagues, friends, family, cooks and chefs who have fed my lifetime's obsession with food. I owe a major debt to my wife, Heather Maisner, with whom I collaborated on no fewer than four cookery books; and also to cookery writer Caroline Conran and Dr Oliver Gillie, a former medical correspondent, who first fuelled my enthusiasm for the theme of this book, healthy, good food. A large number of food writers have been a constant source of inspiration, chief among them, the late Elizabeth David and Jane Grigson; and, alphabetically, Antonio Carluccio, Robert Carrier, Anna del Conte, Ken Hom, Madhur Jaffrey, George Lang, Kenneth Lo, Elisabeth Lambert Ortiz, Sri Owen, Claudia Roden, Egon Ronay, Maria José Sevilla, Paula Wolfert. I also owe a debt to Frances Bissell, Alan Davidson, Sophie Grigson, Harold McGhee, Jill Norman and Tom Stobart, whose reference books I am always consulting.

A number of cooks and chefs were the source of recipes including; Vaughan Archer of the Park Lane Hilton, Gay Bilson of Berowra Waters Inn, Sydney, Maddalena Bonino formerly of 192 Kensington Park Road, Anton Edelmann, the Savoy Hotel, Frédy Girardet of Crissier, Lausanne, Shaun Hill of Gidleigh Park, Chagford, Devon, Bruno Loubet of the Four Seasons, Park Lane, Alain Senderens of Lucas-Carton, Paris, Carla Tomasi formerly of Friths, Roger Vergé of Moulin de Mougins in Provence.

Other sources of recipes include Ayano Crawley, the Covent Garden Soup Company, Ilana Dannheisser, Flora Gardens School (parents contributing to the international evening), Maria Johnson, Julia Lascelles, Fay Maisner, Eva and Andrej Blonski, Namita Panjabi, Ingrid Selberg and Andrew Whitly.

I am also grateful to Marina Knox and Lorraine Tan who typed the manuscript; to my agent Abner Stein; to Sue Hart who edited it and to Rowena Gaunt, whose idea the book was.

Introduction

We may be embarking upon a Golden Age of Cooking. There are now better opportunities to enjoy food in Britain than at any other time in our history. If 'The Good Old Days' ever did exist, then they were only for the wealthy few. Today everyone can draw upon the widest range of produce in the market and the high street.

Two important influences stand out: first, our increasingly adventurous appetite for dishes from around the world, and second, an urgent concern for food which is fresh and healthy.

This book reflects the new optimism. It is a collection of the world's classic dishes which taste good and do you good. They include Spanish paella, Italian risotto, Cajun jambalaya, Indonesian gado gado salad; ratatouille, hummous and falafel; rye breads, cornbreads and chapatis.

In their own countries these are national treasures, mainly based on staple foods. They have stood the test of time, and many have been refined by centuries of practice. A lot of them are already known and appreciated here, though not always, perhaps, in their authentic richness.

We have been changing our style of eating steadily over the last decade. Once we had the habit of demanding only food which was quick, easy and convenient; now we are insisting that it should also be tasty, fresh and healthy.

The trend towards eating fresh food has been put in place by the consumer, and not without a struggle. It is in the food-processing industry's interest to defend profit margins of mass-produced, heavily-processed, cheap food, and if we want something better we have to fight for it.

Take bread, our staple food. Our bread industry pursued the goal of a cheap loaf, and achieved it. We pay only 50p for a 2 lb loaf of bread, against £1.25 in Belgium and £1.50 in

Germany. But there is no joy in eating a loaf of factory-made, sliced white bread and, gradually, sales of this kind of white bread have dropped. Yet over the last 15 years sales of wholemeal bread have increased six-fold.

It is the bread baked for taste and flavour (not for cheapness) which is increasing in popularity – continental loaves such as ciabatta, olive breads and sourdough breads. Speciality breads are the second most important source of profit in one of the big five supermarket chains, after cigarettes and alcohol.

The process of changing the habits of a lifetime is sometimes like trying to turn round an ocean liner in mid-Atlantic: you turn the wheel and nothing happens, and then, eventually, new horizons open up. This is what is happening now.

No country in the world, not even the United States, is as hospitable to influences from abroad. We have now started to colonise cuisines with the enthusiasm we once reserved for annexing an empire. We plunder from near and far, but this is part of a long tradition.

For example, we have enjoyed a love affair with French cuisine since Norman times, renewed every century. The greatest French cook, Carême, father of French *haute cuisine*, cooked for the Prince Regent in the eighteenth century; Auguste Escoffier, author of the greatest collection of classical French recipes, was chef at London's Savoy Hotel in the 1890s.

We also flirt with Italian food, and these days eat more pasta than ever before. Our affairs with foreign cuisines are actually embarrassingly numerous. Our liaison with the Raj produced many Indian high street restaurants, and our presence in Hong Kong for more than a century gave us just as many Chinese restaurants and take-away outlets. Closer to home, our links with Cyprus opened up the Middle East, and brought us Greek–Cypriot cooking. Hummus, taramasalata and kebabs are now part of the British heritage.

This is only the tip of the multicultural iceberg. London, for example, is host to restaurants representing all the world's major cuisines, and many minor ones. There are Thai, Vietnamese, Indonesian, Malaysian, Burmese, Korean and Japanese restaurants. You can eat Turkish, Lebanese, Israeli, Egyptian, Iraqui, Tunisian, Algerian and Moroccan food. You can eat your way across Europe, through Russia, Poland, Germany, Hungary, Switzerland, Sweden and Spain as well as Italy and France. You can eat Texan, Cajun and Californian food, or Brazilian or Mexican.

Cookery books on foreign food were a trickle in the 1930s, and now they are a flood-tide. But it is television which has brought these cultures into the living room. The Indian actress and writer Maddhur Jaffrey was first to demystify Indian cooking when she demonstrated how to make curries at home using freshly ground spices. Since then television has gone the whole hog. Is there any cuisine apart from Berber and Inuit which we haven't examined in fine detail?

Enthused by what we see, here in Britain, we can buy all the ingredients required. This wouldn't be true in France, Germany or Scandanavia. This is because supermarket buyers have simply stepped into the shoes of the old merchant-adventurers who brought back booty from all corners of the earth.

Cooking for good health

Cooking our way around the world fits in very comfortably with modern ideas on healthy eating. In the 1970s, nutritionists had to fight to alert people to the dangers of the British diet. It contained too much fat, leading to premature heart disease, and also too much sugar, causing obesity and consequent chronic illness, and dental decay.

The message was finally accepted in the 1980s. Rows of 'Lo-fat', 'Hi-fibre', 'No-cholesterol', 'Sugar-reduced', 'Salt-free' items appeared on supermarket shelves. Produce claimed 'No additives' or 'No tartrazine'. New sections sold organic produce grown without chemical fertilisers or pesticides.

But the health message was confusing. It didn't represent nutritional sense so much as food phobia. Every packet of food carried nutritional information, such as the number of calories, volume of protein, fat and carbohydrate per 100 g serving, but who except other nutritionists were able to interpret it?

Some messages are actually misleading: 'Hi-fibre', 'Lo-fat', 'Lo-sugar' – 'high' and 'low' compared to what? The villain of the piece is not the pork chop (where you can trim off external fat) but the pork pie (which is loaded with extra fat in the meat filling and in the pie crust). Or consider the invisible amounts of fat (or sugar) concealed in biscuits, ice-creams, chocolate bars, snacks, canned meats and pâtés.

No wonder people are bewildered as to what is safe to eat or drink, whether it's beef, chicken, eggs or apples; alcohol, coffee, milk or water. For a time, it seemed that every health, safety, or nutrition warning was immediately contradicted by a counter-claim. What was one to believe?

The Healthy Eating Pyramid

Happily, the emphasis of the 1990s is shifting to a calmer view of eating. The World Health Organisation led the way in 1991 when they recommended simply that we should eat more starchy foods (so-called 'complex carbohydrates' such as bread, rice, pasta and potatoes), as opposed to 'refined carbohydrates' such as sugar. They also urged us to eat more fruit and vegetables.

The British government finally took up the issue in 1992 and, based on the findings of the Committee on Medical Aspects of Food Policy (COMA), laid down national goals to reduce consumption of saturated fats and eat more carbohydrates.

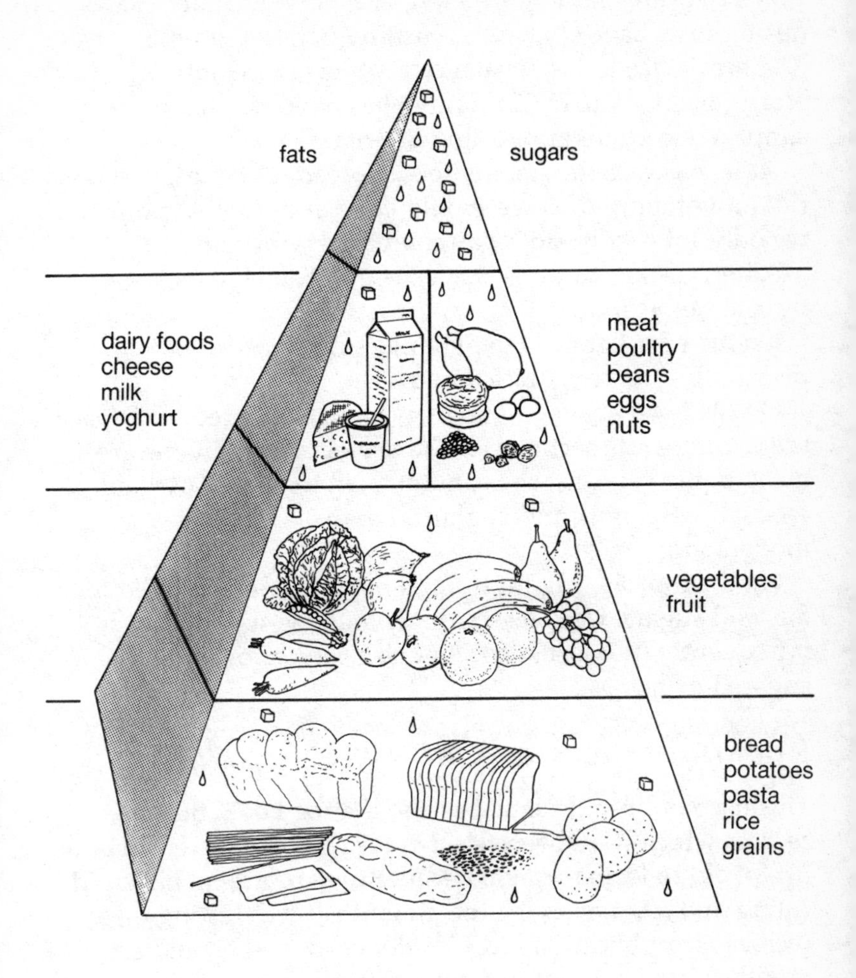

KEY: Fat (naturally occurring and added)

sugars (added)

These symbols show fats, oils and added sugars in foods.

Positive aims replace negative ones. In the United States nutritionists have evolved a 'Healthy Eating Pyramid', a graphic device to teach balanced eating. The Dunn Nutritional Centre in Cambridge has now adapted this simple concept for application in Britain.

At its base are the starchy foods (bread, potatoes, pasta, rice and other grains) we should eat plentifully. At present we only eat 4 oz bread a day compared with some Mediterranean countries, such as Greece, where they eat three times as much.

On the next floor of the pyramid, also to be eaten plentifully, are vegetables and fruit.

On the level above, occupying dramatically reduced space, are two separate sections for the protein foods: in one are meat, poultry, beans, eggs and nuts; in the other are dairy foods, cheese, milk and yoghurt. Eat these foods in moderation.

On the top, sharing the attic, is the tiny space allotted for fats and sugars. Use fats sparingly and use sugars infrequently (not just sugar, but also confectionery and sugared drinks).

Cooking to lose weight, and stay slim

This has not been designed as a slimming book. But the recipes which have been selected for inclusion here can be a useful aid to losing weight because they represent balanced eating. In fact, during the three months I was testing these recipes for publication I lost 1½ stones in weight, and six months later I had not put it back on.

This style of dieting suits those of us who love food, but find the rigours of self-denial unappealing. When you focus on starchy foods, the so-called 'complex carbohydrates', as the basis of your eating, you can continue to enjoy your food and satisfy your appetite. If we were consigned to the monotony of eating packs of white, sliced bread this wouldn't be any fun at all but happily, as the selection of recipes in this book shows, most people in the world have too high a regard for their taste buds to think of that.

Of course, you need a certain amount of conscious effort and self-discipline to lose weight, even following a sensible eating pattern. The scales and common sense will check your occasional excesses. But you can speed up the process if you take a bit more exercise. Physical activity raises your metabolic rate and afterwards induces a feeling of well-being, not the tortured satisfaction that comes from starving yourself thinner.

You achieve greater self-esteem from eating well than you do by starving yourself. Yet, in the United States the slimming business is, apparently, the fifth largest industry in the country. Moreover, something like 90% of slimmers return to their original weight when they come off calorie-controlled diets, and some even go up. Isn't it better to eat well, and reduce your weight very gradually?

Some knowledge of calories is helpful, but I have to say, that after all these years involved in the subject, the only figures I carry in my head are for Stilton, crinkle chips and salted roast nuts, which are a thousand calories a half pound; and for celery, watercress and carrot, which I remember as roughly zero calories. (I have rounded up the figures to the nearest thousand for ease of remembering.)

This view of eating opens up rich fields of opportunity. I've mentioned the revolution in bread, and our longing for handmade loaves prepared with slow-matured dough, giving more texture and flavour. There are plenty of good bread recipes in this book. And we can thank the wholefood movement for introducing us to a large range of dried beans, pulses, grains and flours. Vegetables, too, are another success story of our time. Potatoes and root vegetables lend themselves to infinite variations, on their own or combined in soups and stews. We can hardly keep up with the pace of change in the marketplace, encouraging us to widen our repertoire of recipes to keep up.

This collection of recipes is derived from many sources: from colleagues in the food world I've campaigned with, and food writers I've collaborated with; from my travels, both for my work, and on holiday; from chefs and cooks in restaurants; from family and friends; from neighbours and from the parents of my children's primary school whose annual international evening is a gastronomic event of great merit.

This book of recipes reflects the way I eat. And although the dishes are summoned from the four corners of the world, I have come to think of them as my own.

How to use the book

This round-the-world Cooks' Tour takes in over 50 countries, and they are set out on page 265 together with their recipes.

In presenting this selection of the world's tastiest, most healthful dishes, the book has been divided into six main areas. Each is grouped around specific staple foods and basic ingredients. The first section gives recipes for vegetables and potatoes; followed by beans and pulses, followed by breads, pastry and pasta; grains (such as rice and bulgar); meat, fish and dairy; finally come fruit and puddings, and relishes.

Each section is self-contained. For ease of reference, the order of the recipes follows that of a menu, where relevant: soups, then starters, followed by salads, side-dishes and main dishes.

Measurements

The quantities given for most recipes in this book are approximate. In every country the cook will vary the quantity of ingredients according to availability of ingredients, personal taste and the mood of the moment. Instructions for breadmaking are more critical but, even so, you can get differing results from flour bought at different times in different places, the quality of water varies, and oven temperatures do not always conform to the makers' promise.

Although supermarkets are beginning to go metric and mark produce such as butter and flour in grams, this is still not the custom in street markets or high street grocers, greengrocers, butchers and fishmongers. They cling to pounds and ounces. And although it is over 20 years since we officially embraced the metric system straw polls which I conduct each year suggest that the nation still cooks in pounds and ounces. This book conforms to that usage. It's easy to think of 1 lb as 500 g, and 1 lb as 2 kilos, but this is not precisely so and, rather than fuss around with parallel measures which do not produce rounded figures, here is a scale of reference for the Europeans among us.

Weights		**Volume**			**Measurements**	
1 lb	450 g	1¾ pint	35 fl oz	1 litre	12 inches	30 cm
½ lb	225 g	1 pint	20 fl oz	570 ml	6 inches	15 cm
¼ lb	110 g	½ pint	10 fl oz	290 ml	2 inches	5 cm
2 oz	55 g	¼ pint	5 fl oz	150 ml	1 inch	2.5 cm
1 oz	30 g	2 tablespoons	2 fl oz	56 ml		
½ oz	15 g	1 tablespoon	1 fl oz	28 ml		

The recipes

Some recipes are quick and easy (noodles, pasta, and as quick as microwaving). But it's an insult to people's intelligence to suggest they should never take trouble to do anything which takes more than a few minutes. Some are long, slow and economical (beans, for example – but if you make a large amount you can use them in different ways in salads and stews for a week afterwards). Some require little skill but some patience – efforts which will be rewarded as in the making of a sourdough bread. Most have ingredients which are easily available. Only a few have esoteric spices such as the Thai *kaffir lime* leaves or the Indonesian shrimp paste, *baluchan*, and any cook will know to improvise to approximate to the character and flavour of the dish.

This is a collection of recipes from around the world which taste good, and which I believe fit in to today's notions of healthy, balanced eating. It is not essentially a book of healthy recipes designed for dieters, though you can if you wish to reduce weight easily and safely eating along these lines, because the dishes are both filling and nutritious. It's a matter of your own judgement to increase or decrease portions, or to add or subtract ingredients.

Mostly the cooking medium is a vegetable oil which is unsaturated, but where relevant, the traditional fat in the countries of origin (lard in China, butter in France, *ghee* in India) is indicated because it can contribute to a special flavour. In Russia, for example, unsaturated sunflower oil happens to be preferred because it's easily available and Russians like the flavour. In some parts of the tropics the most easily available cooking fat is *dende* (palm oil) and coconut oil, both of which are heavily saturated. I haven't included dishes using them: they would have a place in a coronary killer collection, if ever there was a call for one.

Oil and fat, whether unsaturated or not, supply twice as many calories as starchy carbohydrates. So even unsaturated oils, used to excess, contribute to obesity and make you fat. There's a belief abroad that if a little does you good, a lot must be better, as exemplified by the status of olive oil. If only this were so!

1

VEGETABLES AND POTATOES

The recipes in this section have been chosen from cultures which regard vegetables as something special, not as one of the 'two veg' that we think to put with 'meat'. You don't need to be a vegetarian to welcome the change in attitude towards vegetables. We have broken free at last from an extraordinary tradition of treating them as second class citizens, carelessly cooking them till the life and nourishment is knocked out of them.

First are the soups: cold soups and light summer soups; then the heavier winter soups which, with plenty of good bread, are often substantial enough to make a meal in themselves.

These are followed by a section on vegetables as starters, appetisers and then substantial salads which can also make a main course if required.

Finally, a section on potatoes, which are half-way between a vegetable and a starchy staple, bursting with the vitamin C of one, and the filling goodness of the other.

SPAIN

Almond Soup
Sopa de Almendras

A nourishing, cooling and elegant chilled soup from Andalucia, echoing the influence of Moorish occupation many centuries ago. Sometimes it's served prettily with a red rose petal floating in each bowl, or sometimes sprinkled with rose petals.

SERVES 4

6 oz blanched almonds
1 large glass dry white wine
1 clove garlic
2 tablespoons mild olive oil
about 20 white grapes
(generous) 1 pint water
salt
ice-cubes

- Crush the almonds and garlic together in either a mortar or an electric blender.
- Gradually add the water, olive oil and wine, and salt to taste.
- When you have a smooth consistency, your soup is ready.
- Add the peeled, stoned and halved grapes and some ice-cubes just before serving.

SPAIN

Gazpacho

Ever since Carmen Mauro knocked out two policemen with a lethal jug of gazpacho in Pedro Almodóvar's *Women on the Edge of a Nervous Breakdown*, the popular, Spanish national soup has taken a leap in the nation's estimation, being voted the favourite first course in a newspaper poll. At its best, it is a sensationally richly-flavoured cocktail of sweet tomatoes, green peppers, mild Spanish onions, hot, raw garlic and cooling cucumber. Vary the ingredients to your taste, if you prefer.

SERVES 4

4 large tomatoes, skinned and chopped
½ cucumber, peeled
1 green pepper, seeded and chopped
1 onion, finely chopped
2 tablespoons stale white breadcrumbs
8 almonds, crushed
1 tablespoon olive oil
1 tablespoon vinegar
salt and white pepper

- Soak the breadcrumbs in the oil and vinegar for about 1 hour, then squeeze dry.
- Crush all the vegetables (reserving just a little of each for the garnish) to a purée, either in a mortar, which is the traditional way, or in an electric blender.
- Add the seasoning and the crushed almonds and breadcrumbs, and dilute with cold water to the desired consistency, making about 1¾ pints of soup.
- Cover and put in a cool place or refrigerator, to chill.
- Ice-cubes may be added just before serving.
- Serve with diced cucumber, red and green pepper, chopped tomato, chopped hard-boiled egg and finely sliced onion – any, or all, served separately, in small bowls.

ITALY

Tuscan Bread Salad
Panzanella

A surprisingly refreshing, rustic dish, half-way between a soup and a salad, which has affinities with Spanish gazpacho. It is a perfect vehicle for those stale pieces of good sourdough bread or country breads, peasant fare for which we now pay a premium.

SERVES 4

4 very thick slices two-day-old country bread
4 large, ripe tomatoes, skinned and chopped
½ cucumber, peeled and diced
1 green pepper, deseeded and diced
½ bulb fennel, cubed
1 bunch spring onions (or 1 medium onion, finely chopped)
fresh herbs, such as basil or rocket
4 tablespoons olive oil
1 tablespoon white wine vinegar
salt and pepper

- Soak the bread in water for 30 minutes.
- Squeeze dry using your hands.
- Put it in a salad bowl with all the ingredients, mixing well.
- You can if you wish, garnish with anchovies and a few black olives.

UKRAINE

Cherry Soup

Sup Vishni

Fruit soups are served hot and cold in the Ukraine, where the famous fertile, black earth nourishes grain crops, vegetables and orchards in abundance.

SERVES 4

1 lb sweet, dark cherries (stoned)
1 lemon, sliced (with the peel)
1 large glass sweet white wine
2 pints water
1 dessertspoon cornflour
2 oz sugar (or to taste)
½ stick cinnamon

For the garnish
sour cream, to taste

- Put half the cherries in a pan with the water. Bring to the boil and simmer until just tender.
- Strain into another pan, rubbing the cherry flesh through a sieve, or purée it in a blender.
- Return the soup to the heat. Add the cinnamon, lemon and remaining cherries. Simmer for 3–4 minutes.
- Add the sugar and all but 2 tablespoons of the wine. Simmer, stirring, until the sugar is dissolved.
- Dilute the cornflour with the remaining wine and blend this into the soup.
- As soon as the soup thickens, remove from the heat and serve with sour cream.
- In the Ukraine it would be accompanied by rusks.

AZERBAIJAN

Yoghurt Soup
Kavkazsky Sup

The large number of inhabitants of the Caucasus who lived to be centenarians put it all down to a healthy diet based on yoghurt. Obviously there were other factors, but natural yoghurt continues to inspire many. This is a cold soup, very refreshing in the summer, similar in character to certain kinds of Indian *raita*.

SERVES 4

½ lb cucumber, peeled and diced
1 pint carton or live or natural yoghurt
1 pint water
1 tablespoon extra virgin olive oil
1 tablespoon white wine vinegar
1 clove garlic
1 heaped tablespoon chopped, fresh mint
salt

- Put the diced cucumber in a dish, sprinkle with salt and leave for 30 minutes.
- Slice the garlic and with it rub the inside of a bowl large enough to take all the ingredients.
- Sprinkle in the vinegar and rinse the bowl with it.
- Spoon the yoghurt and water into this vinegar- and garlic-flavoured bowl and stir to thin it, adding 2–3 tablespoons extra water, if necessary.
- Drain the cucumbers, add to the yoghurt, mix and chill.
- Blend in the olive oil, a few drops at a time.
- Chill, sprinkle with the mint and serve.

FRANCE

Vichyssoise

This creamy, smooth classic of the French kitchen is delicious eaten hot, though it is usually chilled. It capitalises on the delicate silky smoothness of gently cooked white of leek. It is just as delicious with a little less cream than the original version, which is given here.

SERVES 6

1 medium onion, chopped
2 whites of leeks
1 lb old potatoes
3 pints veal or chicken stock
½ pint double cream
1 tablespoon chives, chopped

- Sweat the onions in a saucepan with a little butter for 5 minutes, without letting them brown.
- Add the chopped leeks, peeled potatoes and stock.
- Allow the potatoes to cook then pass them through a fine sieve.
- When thoroughly cold, add the double cream and chives. A little milk may be added if the consistency is too thick.
- Season with salt to taste.
- Instead of cream, you can beat in a choice of lower fat alternatives, fromage frais or plain yoghurt.

SPAIN

Garlic Soup

Sopa de Ajo

Spain has many versions of garlic soup. At its simplest, it is a dramatic way to avert the pangs of hunger since the garlic fills and satisfies the palate. It is often poured on to dry bread. In this version it is thickened and enriched by being poured, off the heat, over beaten egg. Modern milder versions of garlic soup are made by boiling the garlic rather than frying it.

SERVES 4

4–6 large cloves garlic, peeled and thinly sliced
4 tablespoons olive oil
4 thick slices 2- or 3-day old good, white bread
2 pints water
1 teaspoon sea salt
freshly grated black pepper
yolks of 2 eggs, beaten

- Fry the garlic very slowly in the oil till it turns a nutty brown but does not burn (you can discard or retain the garlic at this stage, as you prefer).
- Crumble the bread and toss in the pan to soak up the flavours.
- Transfer to a saucepan, cover with boiling water and simmer for 20 minutes. Pour the soup into a bowl containing the egg yolks, beating vigorously. Add pepper and salt as required.
- You can cook the garlic without the bread for a clearer, thinner result, and serve it with garlic croutons instead.
- You can make a clear soup with the garlic and after adjusting the flavourings, slip a raw egg into each bowl and eat it semi-poached.
- An altogether richer soup can be made by substituting light stock for water.

FINLAND

Spring Vegetable Soup

Kesakeitto

Finland is not renowned for its standard of cooking any more than its health record, though it was one of the first north European countries to recognise that its high rate of heart disease might be due to a diet high in animal fats. It is improving on both counts, and this delicious summer soup is an example. It was passed on to me by Michelin-starred chef Shaun Hill, whose wife is Finnish.

SERVES 4

1 small cauliflower, cut into florets
4 small carrots, peeled and cut into 1 inch pieces
4 oz new potatoes, scrubbed and cut into 1 inch pieces
4 oz fresh peas
1 pint milk
1 pint water
few leaves fresh spinach, shredded
1 tablespoon plain flour
1 tablespoon fresh parsley and dill, finely chopped
1 teaspoon salt

- Cook the cauliflower, potatoes and carrots in salted water for 5 minutes.
- Add the peas and spinach and cook 5 minutes more.
- Whisk the milk and flour together, and add it to the pan, stirring well. Bring it to the boil, lower the heat, and simmer for 3 or 4 minutes to remove the floury taste.
- Add the dill and parsley moments before serving.

NORWAY

Cauliflower Soup

Blomkälsuppe

A seasonal, summer soup. A typical soup flavouring, which is used especially in neighbouring Denmark, is the Nordic version of a bouquet garni – a bunch of celery leaves, leek leaves and parsley stalks, tied with a string, called a *suppevisk.*

SERVES 6

1 medium cauliflower separated in florets
1 tablespoon olive oil (or butter)
2 tablespoons single cream
3 pints light chicken or veal stock
1 tablespoon plain flour
suppevisk (see above)
1 teaspoon paprika
1 teaspoon salt

- Divide the cauliflower into florets and simmer in the stock with the suppevisk till tender, about 10 minutes.
- Remove with a perforated spoon and keep warm in a dish. Reserve the stock.
- In a saucepan, cook the oil (or butter) with the flour gently for a few minutes, then pour in the cauliflower-flavoured stock slowly, still stirring.
- In a separate bowl, mix the egg yolks with the cream, add a little of the soup drop by drop, and return this mixture to the soup.
- Add the cauliflower pieces and heat gently, but do not let the soup boil or it will curdle.
- Serve in individual bowls and sprinkle each with a little paprika.

ECUADOR

Sopa de Papas

In Ecuador, and neighbouring Peru, the grain prized by the mountain Indians is *quinoa,* a seed-like millet. It is a complex carbohydrate, high in protein.

Quinoa absorbs double its weight in water as it cooks. Four ounces of quinoa, simmered in 8 fluid ounces of water (or stock) produces a substantial substitute for rice or potatoes as an alternative accompaniment to a main course, such as a vegetable stew, and adds interesting texture to modest potato soups, their staple food, when eked out with what small amounts of meat, game and fowl become available. Coypu, a large rodent, was on the menu when I visited Ecuador.

SERVES 4

½ lb potatoes, chopped and diced small
1½ pints water (or stock, a Western improvement)
½ pint milk
½ onion, chopped fine
1 oz quinoa (health food stores sell it)
salt and pepper

- To make this filling potato soup, simmer the potatoes, onions and quinoa in the water and milk mixture for 20 minutes, seasoning well. (The quinoa adds a chewy texture.)
- Stock can be substituted for water.
- It can be also enriched with several peeled cloves of garlic, cooked with the potatoes, then crushed when cooked through.
- It can be spiced up with chilli sauce and soy sauce, or improved with fresh chopped herbs.

COLOMBIA

Chicken Potato and Sweet Corn Soup

Ajiaco Bogotano

This chicken and potato soup is a family favourite in Colombia. It is only worth making when you have real chicken stock – make by simmering the chopped bones left over from a roast chicken, with chopped onion, carrot (put in celery if you want) for 2 hours, and straining. Or you can buy chicken wings for the express purpose of making stock.

SERVES 4

¾ lb potatoes, diced into ½ inch cubes
1 onion
4 oz carrot, grated
2 oz sweetcorn
6 oz chicken, skinned, diced
2 pints chicken stock (home-made)
2 tablespoons single cream (or fromage frais)
rounded teaspoon cumin seeds
salt and white pepper

For the garnish
sour cream
slices of avocado pear
capers

- Place the onion, two-thirds of the potato, chicken, chicken stock, salt and pepper in a large pan. Bring to the boil, cover and simmer gently until the potato is soft and the chicken is cooked.
- Pour into the blender and process until smooth.
- Return the mixture to the pan and add the cumin seeds, carrot, sweetcorn and remaining potato. Cover and simmer for 5–10 minutes, until the potato is cooked.
- Add the cream and serve with thin slices of avocado, capers and a dollop of sour cream.

FRANCE

Pea and Potato Soup
Potage au Petits Pois

This thick soup becomes a filling one-pot meal with the addition of a slice of French bread and a poached egg. It is in the peasant tradition of Provence.

SERVES 4

2 lb fresh peas in the pod, or 1 lb frozen peas
5–6 large new potatoes, waxy yellow ones if possible
1 onion, chopped
3 tablespoons olive oil
1¾ pints boiling water
3 cloves garlic, peeled and crushed
bouquet bay, thyme, fennel and parsley
salt and pepper
pinch saffron
4 eggs
4 slices French bread

- Shell the peas and peel the potatoes.
- Soften the onion over a gentle heat in the oil, without browning.
- Add the potatoes, cut into slices about ½ inch thick, and stir them in, without letting them brown.
- Add the boiling water and the peas, the garlic and the bouquet of herbs.
- Season with salt, pepper and saffron. Cover the pan and simmer slowly.
- When the potatoes are soft, break the eggs into the pan one at a time, and poach gently, till done – a few minutes only.
- Put a slice of bread in each soup plate and spoon an egg and some soup on to it, or serve the bread separately.
- In Provence they might season it with a spoonful of garlic-flavoured mayonnaise called *aioli*.

CHINA

Hot and Sour Soup

This is one of the speediest and most economical of soups, yet it is packed with goodness and sensational flavours. It's basically an assembly job; once you have the ingredients to hand, it's made in 5 minutes. Sometimes it is served with slices of bean curd, providing extra protein; prawns (or shrimps) are optional. Pork is usually used, though they often use beef (and a beef stock) in the Szechuan province, where the dish may also be a little hotter. You could also, if you wish, add a little finely cut bamboo shoot to add to the authenticity.

SERVES 4

2 oz lean pork (or beef), cut into fine shreds
2 oz shelled prawns
1½ pints chicken stock
1 oz Chinese dried mushrooms
3 tablespoons Chinese vinegar or cider vinegar
2 teaspoons sugar
1 tablespoon dark soy sauce
1 teaspoon chilli oil (or tabasco sauce)
1 tablespoon cornflour dissolved in 2 tablespoons cold water
1 egg, beaten
2 teaspoons sesame oil
2 spring onions, chopped finely
white pepper

- Soak the mushrooms in hot water for 30 minutes, drain, discarding the stems but reserving the liquid, and chop finely.
- Drop the shredded pork into boiling water, and cook for a minute, until a scum forms. Rinse in a sieve under the cold tap.
- Heat the chicken stock, adding the mushrooms, soy sauce, chilli oil, pepper, vinegar and sugar and simmer for a few minutes.

- Stir in the cornflour paste to give the soup a little texture.
- Add the pork (or beef), the prawns, and pour in the beaten egg slowly, stirring steadily.
- As the egg sets, add a splash of sesame oil and serve at once, piping hot, with spring onions sprinkled on top.

INDONESIA

Spicy Vegetable Soup

A thin, vegetable soup with clear chicken stock, with dramatic sweet, sour and spicy notes. The hot chilli is balanced by soothing coconut milk. This can be bought in tins. If it's dried, make an infusion by steeping the coconut in boiling water for 20 minutes, and then straining.

SERVES 4

1 large onion
2 large carrots
2 sticks celery
1 small leek
handful green beans
2 pints home-made chicken stock
seasoning
1 clove garlic
1–2 chilli peppers (green or dried and pounded)
1 teaspoon turmeric
slice fresh green ginger, the size of a marble (optional)
1 lemon
2 teaspoons brown sugar
4 tablespoons desiccated coconut

- Peel the vegetables and cut into thin strips, but not quite as small as julienne matchsticks.
- Make ½ pint of coconut milk by steeping 4 tablespoons desiccated coconut in ½ pint boiling water, and straining after 15 minutes.

- Gently fry a tablespoon of the onion, very finely chopped, in a very little oil until soft.
- Add the crushed garlic, ginger and finely crushed green chillies (or powdered chilli or chilli sauce) and the turmeric. Stirring with a wooden spoon, heat through without burning until it is a sticky paste.
- Heat the stock with the coconut milk and the spicy paste, add the sugar and chopped vegetables and simmer slowly for 30 minutes.
- Check for seasoning. You can add soya sauce instead of salt for a more characteristic flavour.
- Before serving, stir in the juice of a lemon.

GEORGIA

Almond Soup

The independent southern countries of what used to be the USSR gave a centuries-old cuisine of remarkable sophistication. This almond soup is a by-product of the cooking of a piece of veal, to be served cold as another course, probably the following day, with cold, cooked vegetables and a mayonnaise.

SERVES 4

2 pints good veal stock, seasoned with lemon peel
6 oz ground almonds
4 hard-boiled eggs, yolks only
1 teaspoon salt
ground white pepper

- Halve the hard-boiled eggs and remove the yolks, keeping the whites for another dish, as stuffing or garnish.
- Combine the yolks, ground almonds, salt and remaining lemon rind and pound to a paste in a mortar or put through a blender.

- Dilute the mixture with a cupful of stock, adding a little at a time.
- Bring the rest of the stock to the boil.
- Add the almond mixture, blend thoroughly, simmer for 10 minutes and serve.

Veal stock To make the veal stock, leaving a good piece of veal for a cold dish.

1½ lb lean veal	*rind and juice 1 lemon*
1 medium onion, chopped	*1 bay leaf*
2 stalks celery, chopped	

- Put the veal in a saucepan with 2½ pints of water, bring to the boil and skim.
- Cover and simmer for 1 hour.
- Add the onion and celery to the stock, together with the bay leaf, peppercorns and salt, and cook for 1½ hours.
- Chop the lemon rind finely. Add half of it and all the lemon juice to the stock, and continue to simmer for another hour.
- Strain the stock, leave it until cold, then remove all the surface fat.

WEST INDIES

Callaloo Soup

This succulent, nourishing dish goes back to the plantations when slaves made use of foodstuffs not prized by the owners, such as salted pigs tails, crabs from the beach and the green leaves of the eddoe, the starchy tuber used as a root vegetable in the tropics.

The result is a uniquely gooey, soupy, succulent dish which makes West Indians smack their lips in anticipation. There's no need to use pig tails in this recipe, but if you insist on authenticity, they can be purchased from Caribbean stores.

Serve the cracked claws of the crab (and legs if they are large enough) in the soup, to pick over with your fingers.

SERVES 4

1 lb callallo leaves (or Swiss chard or Chinese leaf or even spinach)
4 oz fresh okra pods (ladies' fingers) sliced
4 oz salt pork or bacon (or salted pigs tails) cut into ½ inch pieces
2 medium crabs or ½ lb crab meat (or white fish fillet)
2½ pints chicken stock
1 onion, finely chopped
4 spring onions, chopped
2 cloves garlic, crushed and chopped
2 tablespoons sunflower oil (or 1 oz butter)
pinch thyme
salt and pepper (or cayenne)

- Crack open the crabs and remove the flesh; crack the claws and reserve.
- In a frying pan, gently cook the onion in the oil (or butter) till soft but not brown.

- Cook the salt pork with the onions till the fat starts to run.
- Add the garlic, spring onions and thyme and cook a minute longer.
- Chop the callallo (or green leaves) roughly, and stir into the pan.
- Transfer to a large saucepan, add the stock, bring to the boil, and simmer about 20 minutes, until the pork is tender.
- Add the okra and simmer for another 10 minutes, and finally add the crab (or fish), including the cracked claws, and cook another 5 minutes to blend all the flavours.
- Season with salt (if required) and plenty of freshly milled pepper (or cayenne if preferred).
- Serve with rice, giving each person a claw to extract the meat from.

ENGLAND

Thick Pea Soup

Tasty, nourishing and inexpensive, a north of England classic. Although it's called pea soup it's actually made with yellow lentils.

SERVES 4

1 lb bacon bones (from the rib)
¼ lb yellow lentils
2 small carrots, diced
1 onion, sliced
1½ pints water
pinch salt
pepper

- If the bacon bones are very salty (usually red in colour), leave them to soak for an hour to reduce the salt content.
- Put the carrots and onions in a pan with the bones and water, and simmer with the lid on for 1 hour.
- Remove the bones, add the lentils, and check the seasoning.
- Cook on a low heat till the lentils are soft (30–40 minutes).

UKRAINE

Sorrel and Spinach Soup

Sorrel is a sharp-tasting, lemony leaf, like spinach, usually found in kitchen gardens, seldom in the shops, but in the Ukraine and in some of the Baltic states it is combined with the meatier leaves of spinach to make this shrill-flavoured soup, very high in vitamins and minerals. It needs a little sugar to temper its sour quality.

SERVES 4

½ lb sorrel, chopped
1½ lb spinach, chopped
1–2 potatoes, peeled and diced
1–2 tablespoons lemon juice
2 tablespoons oil (or butter)
1 egg yolk
4 hard-boiled eggs
4 tablespoons sour cream
½ pint milk
1¾ pints stock or water
pinch sugar
sprig parsley, chopped
salt and pepper

- Heat the oil (or butter) in a pan large enough to take all the ingredients. Add the sorrel, spinach and parsley and cook on a low heat, stirring, for 5 minutes.
- Add the stock or water, then the potatoes and season to taste with salt and pepper. Add the sugar, bring to the boil and cover. Reduce the heat and simmer for 25 minutes.
- Strain, keeping the liquid.
- Rub the sorrel, spinach and potatoes through a sieve, or put in a blender, with half the milk, to make a smooth purée.
- Re-heat the stock, add the purée and simmer for a few minutes.
- Dilute the egg yolks with the remaining milk and blend into the soup. Re-heat the soup gently and check the seasoning.
- Remove from the heat, sharpen with lemon juice to taste and serve with a hard-boiled egg in each bowl and a tablespoon of sour cream on top.

USA

Pumpkin Soup

Autumn is the season for pumpkin and squash, and an increasing variety are imported, sweeter, tastier and firmer, than the usual offerings of outsize monsters, grown for Hallowe'en fun. Cinnamon is a typically American flavour beloved by the earliest settlers in New England.

SERVES 4

1 lb cubed pumpkin or butternut squash flesh, or young marrow
1 potato, scrubbed but not peeled
1 pint milk
1 oz butter or olive oil
1 small onion, chopped
pinch ground cinnamon
pinch dried marjoram
nutmeg
pinch sea-salt
1 tablespoon sherry (not too dry)

- Boil the potatoes and cook till soft. Reserve the water.
- Peel the cooled potatoes.
- Gently fry the onion in butter till yellow.
- Add the cinnamon, marjoram, a pinch nutmeg and salt, frying for a minute or two till well blended.
- Cover and cook the pumpkin or squash until it is very tender. Stir occasionally to prevent sticking; add a little of the potato water if the pan becomes too dry.
- When the squash is soft, add the potato with its cooking water and boil for 20 minutes.
- Put the mixture in a blender with the sherry and milk and blend until smooth and velvety or mash it, and press through a sieve with the back of a spoon.
- Add the sherry and milk gradually.
- Taste, adjust the seasoning and keep hot over a low heat.
- Serve with good bread.

RUSSIA

Borscht

Every family has their own recipe for borscht in Russia, Poland and the north of Europe, where beetroot is one of the few vegetables to sustain families the winter through, but everyone agrees on the general need to balance the beetroot's sweetness with acidity, and temper its roughness with a little cream. Because the beetroot loses colour in cooking, the best way to give it a dramatic crimson flush is to simmer a little grated fresh beetroot in stock (or vinegar or lemon juice) and add it during the last 5 minutes cooking.

SERVES 6

1 lb stewing beef
¾ lb white cabbage, shredded
3–4 small beetroot, uncooked
2 carrots, cut into matchstick strips
2 stalks celery
1 large onion, diced
½ lb tomatoes, skinned and sieved
1 tablespoon lemon juice
3 pints water
1 tablespoon red wine vinegar
1 tablespoon sugar
1 tablespoon dill
1 tablespoon chopped parsley
1–2 bay leaves
4–5 allspice seeds
1½ teaspoons salt
½ teaspoon black pepper
sour cream

- Wash and dry the meat and trim off surplus fat.
- Cut the meat into pieces and put it in a saucepan with water. Bring to the boil, skim, reduce the heat, cover and simmer for 45 minutes.
- Reserve 1 beetroot and cut the rest into matchstick-sized strips.
- Add all the chopped vegetables, apart from the reserved beetroot and the tomatoes, to the stock and continue to simmer

for 20–25 minutes.
- Add the sieved tomatoes, vinegar, sugar, bay leaves, salt, pepper and allspice. Cook gently for 15 minutes.
- Grate the reserved beetroot finely.
- Put it in a small pan with a cupful of the stock, simmer for 5 minutes and strain the liquid into the borscht. Check the seasoning, sharpen with the lemon juice and sprinkle with the dill and parsley.
- Serve the sour cream separately, to be added according to personal taste.

PORTUGAL

Cabbage Soup
Caldo Verde

Cabbage, for so long contributing the most valuable memories of institutional cooking in Britain, deserves better, especially as it is a vital source of vitamins A, C and E with their anti-carcinogenic powers. But its flavour, too, is exciting when cooked to enhance its mustardy strength. Use a dark-green cabbage, or Savoy or kale, but not Dutch white.

SERVES 4

1 lb cabbage or kale, finely shredded
1 lb potatoes, peeled and quartered
4 slices cooking sausage
2 tablespoons olive oil
salt and pepper

- Boil the potatoes in about 2 pints salted water until very soft.
- Remove with a slotted spoon, mash thoroughly and return to the liquid in the pan, together with the olive oil.

- Add the shredded cabbage and boil quickly for about 3 minutes, then add the slices of sausage and simmer for another minute or so to heat through.
- Season to taste and serve with a crusty bread.

POLAND

Chicken Soup

It is often the tradition in large, poor families that the men should get the lion's share of the meat. It is a wise mother who stews the meat long enough to extract enough of the essential nutrients, serving the liquid as soup to the children and the meat, drained of nutritional benefit, can then be served to the menfolk. Jewish chicken soup is just such a dish and, with some justification, considered to be a cure for many ills. It is served with dumplings made from maize flour (matzo) called *knaidlach*, or *lokshen* (vermicelli). Sometimes a few ounces of pearl barley are added at the beginning of cooking to add bulk to the soup.

SERVES 6

1 boiling fowl, cut into 6, with giblets
1 onion, peeled but whole
½ lb carrots, scraped, cut into thin rings
1 small turnip, peeled
root of Hamburg parsley, scraped (or parsley stalks, tied with string)
salt and pepper
vermicelli

For the knaidlach (dumplings)
5 tablespoons medium matzo (maize) flour
8 tablespoons boiling water
1 egg
1 level tablespoon clarified chicken fat (or vegetable oil)
salt and pepper

- Put the chicken pieces and giblets in a deep saucepan and completely cover with water, adding the carrots, the whole onion, turnip and parsley.
- Bring to the boil, turn down the heat and with a ladle remove the scum until it stops forming.
- Partly cover the saucepan with a lid, and simmer for 3 hours.
- Remove and discard the onion, turnip and parsley.
- Remove the chicken pieces to be served separately (sometimes roasted, or chopped and served cold with a dressing and salad).
- Chill the soup in the fridge, and remove the fat when it has solidified on top. (You can if you like reserve the fat to make knaidlach.)
- To serve, reheat the soup, and season it with salt and pepper. Add vermicelli and cook for a few minutes till tender. Or serve with knaidlach dumplings.

For the knaidlach

- Mix the dumpling ingredients in a bowl, shaping them with your hands into small balls.
- Cook them in fast boiling water (or in the soup) for a few minutes until they rise to the surface, doubled in size.
- If you have a proper boiling fowl it's also common to add the unformed eggs within the fowl to the soup 5 minutes before serving.

SCOTLAND

Cock-a-Leekie Soup

A thick, glutinous broth, rich in flavour, hugely satisfying in the winter. Scotland's answer to Jewish chicken soup, based on a tough old cock bird which renders its goodness into the soup. It's eaten more like a stew in a wide, flat, soup bowl mopped up with plenty of good bread as a one course meal. It is said that the prunes were designed to add sweetness to counter the sometimes bitter flavour of old leeks.

SERVES 6 TO 8

1 boiling fowl, trussed, with its giblets, heart, liver and neck
2 tablespoons rice
1½ lb leeks, white part only, sliced lengthwise
1 onion, chopped
12 prunes (optional)
salt

- Cover the chicken and giblets with cold water in a saucepan just large enough to contain the bird. Bring to the boil. As the scum rises, keep skimming it off until no more appears.
- Add the leeks, onion, rice and salt to taste. Lower the heat until the liquid is simmering so slowly that the surface just trembles with gently breaking bubbles, and cook for 2–2½ hours.
- Remove the bird and giblets, and serve the soup with the leeks in it. The bird is served as the main course with potatoes and green vegetables.
- To make a really thick soup which is a meal in itself, shred the chicken meat after cooking and return it to the pan.
- For a rich flavour, much liked by the Scots, wash a dozen prunes and add them to the soup when you put the chicken in to simmer.

ITALY

Minestrone

The world's most famous vegetable soup, a thick broth of vegetables and beans which vary according to season. Sweating the small, diced vegetables in *pancetta*, the Italian cured bacon, gives it a special basic flavour which makes it different from other soups. If dried white beans are not used, extra protein (and bulk) is provided by adding 4 oz of macaroni during the last 20 minutes of cooking.

SERVES 4 TO 6

4 oz Italian pancetta, or salt bacon, finely chopped
1 large onion, cut into ¼ inch dice
2 carrots, diced
1 head of celery, diced
8 oz haricot or white beans, soaked overnight (or 1 can white beans)
4 oz French beans, cut small
8 oz shelled peas
1 clove garlic, crushed and chopped
1 can tomatoes, chopped
4 pints water (or stock)
1 tablespoon olive oil
salt
Parmesan cheese
parsley, to garnish

- In a large, heavy pan gently sweat the onions in the pancetta.
- Add the celery, then the carrots, and when they are giving off an appetising smell, stir in the garlic.
- Stir in the tomatoes, beans, peas, and add the water (or stock).
- Bring to the boil, turn down the heat, and simmer for 1½ hours.
- Add salt at the end of cooking.
- You can add a sliced quarter of cabbage during the last half of cooking if the soup is to be served immediately, but not if the minestrone is for re-heating the next day, when instead of improving, as it usually does, it would spoil.
- Serve with grated Parmesan and chopped parsley.

ENGLAND ·

Curried Parsnip Soup

The great English cookery writer Jane Grigson is credited with putting curry to parsnips in a soup. The parsnip is a vegetable which is mysteriously unique to Britain, and curry is an exciting foil for its sweetness, and masks the parsnip's slightly choking smell, which is also destroyed by the traditional method of roasting. Boiled, parsnips loose much of their taste, and require a great deal of butter to bring them to life – 'kind words butter no parsnips'.

SERVES 3 TO 4

¾ lb parsnips, peeled, diced into ¼ inch pieces
1 large potato, boiled
2½ pints water, boiling
1 tablespoon olive oil
1 inch green ginger, crushed, finely chopped
1 green chilli pepper, finely chopped
1 clove garlic, crushed and chopped
1 teaspoon turmeric
1 teaspoon coriander, powdered
½ teaspoon cumin seeds, powdered
sea-salt, pepper
vegetable stock cube (optional)

- Gently fry the parsnip in oil, in a frying pan (preferably non-stick) with a lid, until soft, shaking from time to time. Add the spices, turn up the heat, and cook for 2 minutes, stirring well.
- Mix in the potato, and stir for 1 more minute. Pour on the boiling water, and stir to take up the sticky residue.
- Transfer the soup to a saucepan, add the stock cube and simmer for 15 minutes more with the lid on.
- With a ladle, remove half the contents, and press through a conical sieve or *mouli-légumes* and return to the pan. This gives a thick soup, leaving some sweet, spicy pieces of parsnip whole.

SPAIN

Bean and Sausage Soup
Caldo Gallego

A thick, warming, winter soup, from the cold and wet north-west of Spain, which is a meal in itself, with a nutritious combination of meat and vegetable proteins, and a perfect balance of carbohydrates. In a perfect world, food to nurse you into a hale and hearty old age.

SERVES 4 TO 6

½ lb dried white beans, soaked overnight
1 piece chorizo sausage, about 4 oz
1 knuckle bacon
1 lb peeled potatoes, roughly chopped
1 lb kale or cabbage, shredded
1 onion, chopped
1 oz flour
1 tablespoon olive oil
1 teaspoon paprika

- Drain the soaked beans, put into a large pot with about 3 pints fresh water, bring to the boil and add the chorizo and the knuckle bone.
- Simmer for about 1½ hours, then add the potatoes, the greens and the onion.
- Cover and cook slowly for about another 2 hours, until all the vegetables have disintegrated except the beans, which should keep their shape.
- Just before serving, mix the flour with the olive oil and paprika and stir this in.
- Cook for another 5 minutes.
- Cut up the chorizo, scrape any remaining meat off the knuckle bone and return these to the soup.
- Serve very hot.

GREECE

White Bean Soup
Fasolado

Beans provide nourishing protein in the poorer parts of the Balkans, where this, often known as 'Poor Man's Soup', is regularly on the menu. It is, none the less, appetising and filling. It can be made in advance for convenience, and warmed through.

SERVES 4 TO 6

1 lb dried haricot beans
2 slices celeriac, chopped
2 large onions, chopped
2 large carrots, chopped
2–3 tablespoons tomato paste
5 fl oz olive oil
2 tablespoons flat-leaved parsley, chopped
salt and pepper

- Soak the beans overnight in plenty of cold water to cover.
- Rinse well, put into a large pan with 6 pints cold water and bring to the boil.
- Drain off and discard this water.
- Then pour on the same quantity of fresh water, bring to the boil and simmer very gently over a low heat until the beans are cooked (about 1 hour).
- Add the celeriac, onions, carrots, tomato paste, oil and parsley and continue to cook slowly, for about half an hour, until the beans and vegetables are tender.
- Season with salt and pepper to taste.

POLAND

Barley Soup
Krupnik

Barley was the most commonly-used grain in England for centuries and an Englishman was less likely to be known as John Bull as John Barleycorn. It was the stuff of bread, stews and soups, as well as the main ingredient of ale. Nowadays it is only grown for beer and some lager (they use maize mostly) and as an animal feed. In Poland, however, the grain is still prized as a satisfying ingredient, giving a comforting texture and good nutritional backbone to vegetable broths.

SERVES 4

2 pints beef or chicken stock
2 oz pearl barley
2 onions, sliced
2 carrots, diced
1 parsnip, diced
3 stalks celery, diced
½ lb potatoes, diced
a few diced ceps or porcini, soaked in hot water (or 2 oz fresh mushrooms, diced)
2 tablespoons vegetable oil
1 bay leaf
sprig dill, chopped
salt and pepper

- Soak the barley in water overnight.
- Drain and simmer in 1 pint stock for 1½ hours.
- In a large pan heat the oil and lightly fry the onion.
- Add the barley and its liquid, the rest of the stock and the carrots, parsnip, celery, potatoes, mushrooms and bay leaf.
- Cover and simmer for 30 minutes.
- Season to taste with salt and pepper.
- Serve garnished with the dill. If fresh dill is not available, use parsley.

DENMARK

Beer Soup

Ollebrod

A rye bread soup made with non-alcholoic beer eaten at breakfast – which used to be for Danes what porridge is to the Scots. It echoes the breakfasts of the British labourer for centuries, when he started the day with mild ale and a plate of pottage (a gruel or porridge of rye, barley or wheat grains soaked overnight, then cooked slowly till thick). It's an extremely nourishing and healthy winter dish. The prunes are optional.

SERVES 4

½ lb dark rye bread
1 pint mild ale
¾ pint water
12 prunes, soaked overnight in water
piece of zest of lemon
sugar to taste

- Crumble the bread and soak it in the beer and water mixture for 2 hours.
- Bring it to the boil in a large saucepan, adding the lemon peel, and simmer for 10 minutes till the bread breaks up.
- Strain into a sieve, and press through.
- Reheat, adding the stoned prunes and a little sugar to sweeten, and cook till the prunes are tender and the soup is thick and smooth.
- Serve with milk or cream.
- The soup is sometimes thickened by being poured over a beaten egg (or two) off the heat – don't reheat afterwards, or the eggs will scramble.

TURKEY

Aubergine Purée
Köpuglu

A piquant, savoury dip served as a first course with country bread or with salad. This dish is known all over the Balkans as 'Poor Man's Caviar'. In Turkey, garlic is always present. In Bulgaria, they add garlic and pounded walnut paste. In Serbia, they include diced red peppers. In Romania, they serve it with black olives. Further east, in Turkey and Egypt, there are versions mixed with a little yoghurt, and also a tablespoon or two of tahina paste (ground sesame seeds). But the overall, characteristic flavour of the dish is derived from the bitter taste imparted by charring the skin until black.

SERVES 4

1½ lb aubergines
4 tablespoons olive oil
2 cloves garlic, peeled and crushed
juice 1 lemon
salt and black pepper
parsley, finely chopped

- Grill the aubergines slowly until their skins are charred and blistered all over.
- Split them open and scoop out the flesh.
- Mash the flesh with a wooden spoon or process it in a blender.
- Beat in the oil, garlic and lemon juice.
- Season with salt and pepper.
- Serve on a bowl or plate garnished with parsley.

FRANCE

Tapenade

Intensely strong and piquant paste from the south of France eaten with toasted country bread or, if you like, wholemeal bread.

If you make too much, store the paste in a glass jar in the fridge, covering the top with ¼ inch olive oil. In France sometimes a little raw garlic is also added but you need to be confident about your friends if you include it.

SERVES 2

4 oz black olives, stoned
6 anchovies
1 tablespoon capers
squeeze lemon juice
1 tablespoon extra virgin olive oil

- Put all the ingredients into a blender and mix to a rough, thick paste.
- Serve as a first course with country breads, fresh or lightly toasted.

ITALY

Pan Bagna

Pan Bagna literally means 'soaked bread'.
It's picnic fare bursting with flavour and goodness. Prepare it the night before. In France it is made with a filling exactly the same as the traditional salade Niçoise, so it might have a few more ingredients than those below, such as cucumber, green peppers, sliced, small broad beans, small artichokes and the small, black olives of Nice.

SERVES 4 (AS PART OF A PICNIC)

1 loaf ciabatta bread
2 ripe tomatoes, sliced
6 stoned black olives, chopped
½ onion, sliced
2 hard-boiled eggs, halved
4 tablespoons olive oil
1 tablespoon white wine vinegar
green herbs, such as basil or parsley, chopped
sea-salt, black pepper

- Slice the loaf lengthways.
- Lay one half on its back in a flat dish and sprinkle with the vinegar.
- Arrange the tomatoes, olives, onion and egg on top.
- Sprinkle with the herbs, salt and pepper and drizzle with the oil.
- Replace the top of the bread.
- Put a flat weight on top and leave overnight for the flavours to soak in.

MEXICO

Guacamole

A delicious, cool, green purée made piquant with fresh green chillies, the oiliness of the avocado moistened with juicy tomato. Eat it as a dip with tacos or tortillas or pitta bread or serve it as the centre-piece of a salad.

Keep it in the fridge when made, covered with clingfilm to prevent browning, caused by oxidisation. (Although you can scrape off any brown discolouring.)

SERVES 4

2 ripe avocado pears
1 ripe tomato, skinned and deseeded, chopped
1 green chilli, deseeded, finely chopped
4 spring onions, (whites finely chopped) (or 1 tablespoon chopped onion)
2 or 3 sprigs coriander
1 tablespoon olive oil
juice ½ lime (or lemon)
salt and pepper, cayenne (or paprika)

For the garnish
green spring onion, chopped
cayenne pepper

- Mash the avocado pulp with the lime juice, oil and seasoning, lightly blending the onion, tomato, chilli and coriander.
- Put the mixture in a bowl or return it to the empty avocado shells and cover with clingfilm to prevent browning.
- Garnish with cayenne (or paprika), the green of spring onions, and a few coriander leaves.

INDIA

Spicy Aubergine in Tomato

A pungent, spicy north of India dish which makes an appetising first course. Eat it with Indian naan or chappatis, pitta bread, ciabatta or slices of baguette.

SERVES 4 TO 6

2 lb aubergines
2 large, chopped tomatoes
1 tablespoon tomato paste
1 inch green ginger
6 cloves garlic
2 green chillies
1 teaspoon whole cumin seeds
1 teaspoon whole fennel seeds
2 teaspoons ground coriander seed
½ teaspoon turmeric
2 teaspoons salt
½ pint vegetable oil

- In a blender, whiz the garlic, ginger and chillies with just enough water to make a thin paste.
- Cut the aubergines lengthways into 4, and then cut across into 1 inch thick chunks.
- Heat the oil in a wide pan, and, in batches, fry the aubergines till completely tender and reddish-brown on both sides.
- Lift them out with a slotted spoon, and put into a sieve over a bowl for half an hour, to drain off the surplus oil.
- In the same pan, heat 2 spoonfuls oil, and fry the cumin and fennel seeds for a few seconds, then add the tomatoes, the garlic paste, turmeric and salt. Cook gently, stirring well, for about 10 minutes until the mixture thickens.
- Put the drained aubergines into the tomato sauce, cover the pan and cook gently for 10–15 minutes.
- Serve at once, hot, or leave overnight in the fridge for the flavours to develop.
- Serve cold or warm.

TURKEY

Stuffed Sweet Aubergine
Imam Bayildi

The popularity of this dish may have much to do with its name in Turkish which means 'fainting prince', the Imam having apparently swooned when this sweet delicacy was presented to him. It very easily becomes too rich if the aubergine is allowed to sponge up the excessive amount of oil; the sweetness comes from the aubergine absorbing the sweetness of the gently cooked onions, which is accented by the (optional) Christmassy addition of sultanas and scented allspice. This recipe makes a main course for four people, but it can be prepared as an appetiser for eight (see end of recipe).

SERVES 4

4 long, medium-sized aubergines
4 tablespoons olive oil
2 onions, finely sliced
2 green peppers, seeded and finely sliced
4 cloves garlic (or less), finely chopped
3 medium-sized tomatoes, peeled, seeded and chopped
3 tablespoons parsley, finely chopped (keep 1 spoonful for garnish)
1 teaspoon allspice
2 oz sultanas
salt
freshly ground black pepper
¼ pint water
juice 1 lemon

- Cut a deep slit lengthways down each aubergine, stopping short of the top and base, and place them in a bowl of very salty water for 30 minutes.

- Meanwhile prepare the filling. In a heavy pan heat 2 tablespoons olive oil.
- Gently fry the onions with the green peppers and garlic until soft and melting.
- Then combine them with the tomatoes, parsley, allspice, salt and black pepper, to taste.
- Drain the aubergines, gently squeeze out the moisture with your hands, and dry with paper towels.
- Put the rest of the olive oil in the pan and fry the aubergines, gently turning several times (take care not to spoil the shape) until they begin to soften.
- Take the pan off the heat and turn all the aubergines so the slit is facing upwards. (If you prefer to bake them in the oven, you can transfer them to an oven-proof dish.)
- Force as much filling as possible into the slits, and put any that is left on top.
- Pour on the water and lemon juice.
- Either cook on top of the stove on a very gentle heat, or bake in the oven, preheated at 325°F, 160°C, gas mark 3, for 45 minutes.
- Leave to cool at room temperature, then chill, if you like.
- Best eaten cool or cold, and garnished with parsley.
- Alternatively, to make the dish for 8, as an appetiser, halve the aubergines after they have been soaked. Scoop out the flesh, chop it, and fry it in oil, before blending with the other ingredients. Drizzle with oil before baking in a hot oven for 30 minutes.

FRANCE

Crudités

Michel Guérard, the most innovative French chef of his generation, once told me his favourite taste sensation was a raw, baby radish straight from his kitchen garden, dipped in butter and sea-salt. The teeth crunch into the radish which releases its cargo of mustardy juice. As you crunch the radish, the hot juices explode on to your tongue, mixing with the salt and the melting butter. The French understand the nutritional benefits of raw vegetables, and turn them into taste-treats with their usual expertise.

In restaurants, vegetables such as celeriac are served with a mustardy *sauce remoulade*. Finely-grated carrot is not spurned, served with a sweet-sour vinaigrette of oil, vinegar, Dijon mustard, salt and pepper. In the south of France a plate of sliced green peppers, sliced young carrots, cucumber and celery will be served with garlicky mayonnaise, *aioli*.

This anchovy dressing is served hot with a head of celery, divided.

SERVES 4

1 small tin anchovies
1 head celery
4 tablespoons olive oil

- Put the anchovies and their oil in a small saucepan and heat gently.
- After a few minutes, when they start to dissolve, pound them up, stir in extra olive oil and beat well together. Keep hot until ready to serve.
- Serve the celery with the bowl of anchovy dressing, mopping up the juice with good country bread.

- For added flavour, include a teaspoon of Dijon mustard, a squeeze of lemon juice, and a twist of freshly milled black pepper.
- The Italian *bagna cauda* is a variation on this theme, the addition of garlic giving it extra bite: slice a clove of garlic finely and fry it in olive oil for a few minutes to flavour the oil, but do not let it colour. Serve the anchovy, garlic and oil mixture with a plate of sliced, raw vegetables in season, such as red, yellow and green peppers, fennel and celery.

GREECE

Marinated Mushrooms

A way to add interest to a meal without adding a lot of calories and a particularly delicious appetiser. The mushrooms are marinated in a cooked dressing.

SERVES 4 TO 6

1 lb button mushrooms
¼ pint (5 tablespoons) white wine vinegar
2 tablespoons extra virgin olive oil
1 tablespoon lemon juice
2 cloves garlic, crushed
1 sprig parsley
1 stem thyme
1 bay leaf
4 peppercorns
4 coriander seeds

- Trim the mushrooms, cover with water, a squirt of lemon juice and a pinch of salt, and bring to the boil.
- Simmer gently for 10 minutes. Drain.
- Simmer the oil, vinegar, herbs and spices in a separate pan for 20 minutes.
- Put the mushrooms in a bowl, cover with the marinade, and chill overnight at least, preferably 24 hours, to impregnate the flavours.

YUGOSLAVIA

Leek Salad

Leeks are the aristocrats of the vegetable world whose subtle breeding is understood by gourmets. They add subtlety and smoothness to any soup or broth, but here they figure in all their beauty.

SERVES 4

8 leeks
4 tablespoons olive oil (approximately)
1 tablespoon wine vinegar
black olives, for garnish
salt and pepper

- Clean and trim the leeks, keeping as much of the green as possible.
- Cut into 4 inch lengths and cook gently in simmering, salted water until just tender.
- Drain thoroughly and put in a serving dish.
- Make a dressing with 4 parts oil to 1 part vinegar and pour over the leeks.
- Add a generous seasoning of pepper and garnish with the olives.
- Eat warm, or leave overnight to soak up the juices and eat cold.

ITALY

Tomato and Onion Salad

A marriage of ripe Mediterranean tomatoes and mild sweet onions. If the onions seem to be too fierce after you slice them, plunge them into boiling water, then rinse under a cold tap, and mop dry. Taste, and if still too hot, repeat the process.

SERVES 4

2 lb sweet, ripe tomatoes, sliced into circles
1 large Spanish onion (or 6–8 shallots)
1 stem of mint leaves, chopped
4 tablespoons olive oil
1 tablespoon white wine vinegar
1 small clove garlic, crushed and finely chopped
salt
pinch sugar

- Lay the sliced tomatoes and onions in a shallow, earthenware dish and sprinkle on the mint.
- Beat together the oil, vinegar, garlic, salt and sugar and pour over the salad.
- Leave the salad for 1 hour, for the tomatoes to marinate.
- Put in a cool place, but not the fridge.

USA

Coleslaw

The European immigrants to America, who knew the healthy benefits of raw vegetables, also had no Puritan wish to suffer in the cause of nutrition, and this classic salad is full of crunch and exciting sweet and sour flavours. One of the world's great dishes when prepared with the respect it deserves. A spanking fresh cabbage is essential.

SERVES 6

1 lb white cabbage, tough stalk removed
1 small onion (or 6 spring onions)
2 sticks celery
1 green pepper
1 carrot
1 apple (peeled or unpeeled, to taste)
½ cucumber, peeled and deseeded
parsley

For the dressing
4 oz Greek-style yoghurt or fromage frais
2 tablespoons virgin olive oil
1 tablespoon red wine vinegar
½ tablespoon Dijon mustard
pinch caraway seeds
salt and pepper

- Shred the cabbage finely into a bowl.
- Grate the apple and carrot.
- Finely dice the green pepper, celery and onion.
- Dice the cucumber and put into a saucer, sprinkle with salt, and leave in the fridge for an hour.
- Mix the ingredients for the dressing and combine with the salad.
- Chill for an hour before serving, stirring in the drained cucumber cubes.
- Sprinkle with chopped parsley.

MARTINIQUE

Leyritz Salad

Green bananas are the essential ingredient of this feast of a Caribbean salad from an island whose gastronomic ambitions have been honed by the French. The colours are bright, the textures contrasting, from smooth to crunchy. Serve as a first course at lunch, or as a side salad with cold dishes.

SERVES 4

4 green (unripe) bananas
salt
1 large tomato, skinned, deseeded and coarsely chopped
6 sticks celery, sliced
2 medium carrots, scraped and shredded
1 ripe avocado, peeled, stoned and sliced
lettuce leaves, washed and shaken dry

For the vinaigrette dressing
4 tablespoons olive oil or sunflower oil
1 tablespoon white wine vinegar
1 teaspoon Dijon mustard
1 clove garlic, crushed and chopped
salt and pepper

- Peel the bananas making several cuts lengthways through the skin.
- Put the peeled, whole bananas in a saucepan with salted water. Cook, covered, for 10–15 minutes, or until tender.
- Drain and cool them, then cut into ½ inch slices.
- To prepare the vinaigrette dressing, combine the ingredients and beat till smooth (or put them in a jar with a lid and shake well).
- Line a dish with lettuce.
- In a large bowl toss the ingredients in the vinaigrette dressing, and then arrange the pieces decorously.

USA
Caesar Salad

This is one of the great classic dishes of the United States though it originates in Tijuana, Mexico, on the border close to San Diego. It's exact composition arouses fierce argument, but essentially, its delight resides in its contrasts: the crunchiness of the cold, crisp lettuce and the hot, garlicky fried bread, the slipperiness of the oily dressing and runny egg, and the saltiness of the anchovy and Parmesan cheese. It is sufficient to make a main course, supplemented with good white or wholemeal bread. Uncooked egg yolk will give grounds for doubts in these days of salmonella poisoning (most at risk are small children, pregnant women, and the old or invalid). It can be left out, if necessary.

SERVES 4

2 heads cos lettuce (or heart Webb's lettuce)
4 thick slices bread, crusts removed, cubed
1 can anchovy fillets, drained
juice 1 lemon
yolk 1 egg
2 oz Parmesan cheese, grated
3 cloves garlic
salt and freshly ground black pepper
olive oil for frying

- Wash, mop dry, and chill the lettuces.
- Fry 2 of the garlic cloves, sliced, in a little olive oil.
- Remove the garlic and fry the bread cubes in the oil quickly, to brown the outside to make garlic croutons. Drain them on absorbent paper.
- Rub a salad bowl with the cut side of the remaining clove of garlic.
- Tear the lettuce into pieces and toss into the salad bowl.

- Lightly beat the egg yolk, and stir it into the lettuce leaves, adding the lemon juice, anchovies, salt, pepper and grated cheese.
- Using a wooden salad spoon and fork, coat the leaves, rolling them in a continuous motion.
- Taste to check seasoning.
- Sprinkle with the crunchy garlic croutons and serve.

ITALY

Mixed Vegetable Salad
Insalata di Verduri

A simple Italian peasant salad combining cooked and uncooked vegetables, in the manner of the French *Salade Niçoise*. (You can add hard-boiled eggs and anchovies and omit the cucumber if you want to change the geography to France.)

SERVES 4

4 oz freshly cooked, green beans, cut into 1½ inch lengths
½ lb ripe tomatoes
2 boiled new potatoes, sliced
1 cucumber, sliced
1–2 dozen black olives
4 tablespoons olive oil
1 tablespoon wine vinegar
salt and freshly ground pepper

- Arrange the vegetables on a large platter, sprinkled with the oil, vinegar, salt and pepper.

INDONESIA

Salad with Peanut Dressing
Gado-Gado

It is the spicy peanut sauce which makes this salad of cooked and raw vegetables so delicious. Exactly what you put in it will depend on availability. Shrimp paste is an extremely powerful flavour which is traditionally used in many Indonesian (and Thai) dishes.

SERVES 4

Peanut dressing
4 oz unsalted peanuts, shelled
1 tablespoon groundnut oil
1 onion, finely chopped
1 teaspoon brown sugar
1 clove garlic, crushed
2 green chillies, deseeded and finely chopped
juice of ½ lime (or lemon)
½ pint boiling water
½ teaspoon salt
slice of shrimp paste (terasi or blachan, if available) from oriental shops
oil for frying

- Put the peanuts in a heavy iron or non-stick pan, and cook for 5 minutes over a moderately high heat, shaking, to roast the peanuts to a good brown colour. (You can also fry them in a thin film of oil.)
- Put into a blender or pound in a mortar.
- Fry the onion in a little oil, till soft and starting to brown.
- At the end of the cooking, briefly add the garlic and chillies, then the pungent-smelling shrimp paste, and the salt.
- Stir in the peanuts and then add the boiling water, sugar and lime juice.
- Cook for 2 minutes, stirring, and then leave the mixture to cool.

- If it's too thick, add a little more boiling water to thin it.
- Serve on a mixed salad of raw vegetables, together with vegetables blanched in boiling water or slightly undercooked, then rinsed in cold, running water, to keep their crispness and colour.
- This is a suggested combination which you can vary.

SERVES 4

Salad

2 onions, sliced, fried till brown
8 oz green beans, cut into 1 inch lengths, cooked al dente
8 oz carrots, sliced lengthways into strips, cooked al dente
8 oz sweet (or waxy) potato, lightly boiled, cut into thin slices
8 oz Chinese leaf (or spinach), blanched
8 oz bean sprouts, rinsed, raw
½ cucumber, peeled and sliced
8 radishes, quartered
¼ white cabbage, shredded
2 sliced hard-boiled eggs
leaves of mint, torn

- Arrange the salad decorously, sprinkled with the fried onions, pouring over the dressing, finally garnishing with the mint.

TURKEY

Baked Vegetable Casserole
Türlü Güveç

Türlü Güveç is every bit a Balkan classic as the Provençal ratatouille. *Güveç* means a mixture and *türlü* is the flat, wide, earthenware casserole dish it is cooked in. Although it can be cooked in a pot over a low heat, baking in the oven keeps the juices in the vegetables, resulting in a dish which looks fairly firm and solid, but is rich and juicy as you eat it. As in ratatouille, the triumph of this dish is that the whole is greater than the sum of its ingredients. The recipe varies according to the region and the availability of the ingredients. In Greece garlic is often included, and in Bulgaria green chilli peppers (2 or 3 are enough) are added. In some parts of the Balkans, unripened grapes are used to give a tartness (we once used verjuice, the juice of unripened grapes, in Europe before lemons became available).

SERVES 4 TO 6

1 lb potatoes, cut into small chunks
1 lb onions, chopped
1 lb tomatoes, sliced
1 lb aubergine, cut into cubes
1 lb courgettes, cut into chunky rounds
½ lb green beans, cut into 3
½ lb shelled peas (you can use frozen)
1 green pepper, sliced
bunch chopped parsley
4 oz okra (ladies' fingers) (optional)
2 tablespoons tomato purée
4 tablespoons olive oil
2 teaspoons paprika powder
3 teaspoons salt

- Sprinkle salt on to the aubergine cubes, and leave to drain in a colander for 1 hour.
- Pat the cubes dry with absorbent paper.
- Reserving the tomato slices, mix all the ingredients into a wide, shallow casserole dish, seasoning with salt and paprika and half the oil.
- Arrange the tomato slices on top, and sprinkle with the rest of the oil.
- Cook, uncovered, in an oven pre-heated to 400°F, 200°C, gas mark 7 for 10 minutes, then lower the heat to 375°F, 190°C, gas mark 5 and cook for 1–1½ hours till the vegetables are tender and the tomatoes on top have browned.
- Eat hot or cold with country bread.

FRANCE

Ratatouille

This incomparably delicious summer vegetable stew is as good cold as it is warm. Served with a poached or fried egg on top and good bread it can be also a substantial and satisfying meal. The pleasure in eating it is derived as much from its slippery, satisfying texture as its combination of flavours: melting onions, juicy green peppers, sweet tomatoes, and the catalyst which holds the key to this dish, succulent cubes of tender aubergine, which impart a slight bitterness to balance the sweetness of the other vegetables, while soaking up the mixture of flavours.

There are many ratatouille recipes in the south of France, some of them are long-simmered, lovely, wet stews, others are assembly jobs, in which each vegetable is cooked separately, and combined only at the end to be heated through. This particular recipe is extremely elegant, suitable for the table of a top restaurant. For a rough-and-ready ratatouille you wouldn't chop the vegetables so delicately.

SERVES 4

¾ lb aubergines
½ lb green peppers
½ lb onions
½ lb courgettes
½ lb tomatoes, skinned, deseeded
2 cloves garlic
3 tablespoons olive oil
4 tablespoons water
thyme, salt and pepper

- Cut the onions, peppers, aubergines, courgettes and tomatoes into ¼ inch dice. (The aubergines are not salted and drained).
- In half the oil, fry the onion and green pepper pieces for 8 minutes, until soft. Lift them out with a slotted spoon, and

drain on absorbent paper.

- Sauté the aubergine dice using the rest of the oil, adding 4 tablespoons water and stirring vigorously for 2 minutes. Then add the courgettes and cook for another 5 minutes.
- Combine all the ingredients in the pan, adding the tomato, and cook for 5 minutes more, or longer if you prefer less bite to your vegetables.
- Season with salt and pepper.
- The dish can be served at once, or reheated.

CZECHOSLOVAKIA

Bohemian Cabbage

In Central Europe the cooking of the humble cabbage is raised to an art form. In the two provinces of Czecholslovakia, Moravia and Bohemia, there is a heated debate about whose is the better. This is the Bohemian version.

SERVES 4

2 lb white cabbage
1 small onion, finely chopped
4 fl oz sour cream
1 teaspoon caraway seeds
salt and pepper

- Discard the outer leaves with thick, tough stalks. Wash the cabbage and cut it into quarters, then shred it finely.
- Put it into a large pan and add the salt, pepper, caraway seeds and onion with enough water to cover the bottom of the pan to prevent burning. Cover and cook the cabbage over a low heat until tender (30–45 minutes) stirring from time to time. The cabbage should be very soft.
- Just before serving, add the sour cream, stir again and continue cooking until the cream is hot.
- Serve with a main course, such as duck, goose or boiled ham.

RUSSIA

Stuffed Cabbage

This is a classic staple from north to south of Russia, and is both nourishing and tasty. The cooking technique apparently dates back to Tartar cooking in the fourteenth century.

Use substantial, hard white (Dutch) cabbage. The stuffing can be made with minced beef, lamb, pork or veal (although in other parts of Europe, especially France, stuffed cabbage usually means pork). To economise on meat or, indeed, if you prefer it this way, incorporate more breadcrumbs (or uncooked rice or bulgar grains) into the stuffing. It is best when it's made the day before and the flavours allowed to mature overnight. It's so good you may decide it's very little trouble to make double quantities and freeze half.

SERVES 4

1 medium-sized, hard white cabbage
1 lb minced beef, lamb or veal
1 onion, finely chopped
2 oz breadcrumbs or 2 slices bread, soaked in water, squeezed
1 tablespoon tomato paste or ketchup
1 tablespoon chopped parsley
pinch thyme or sage
salt and pepper

The cooking sauce
3 cans chopped tomatoes
1 tablespoon tomato paste (or ketchup)
1 tablespoon brown sugar
juice 1 lemon
water

- Remove the tough outer leaves and core from the cabbage, then cook in a steamer for 10 minutes to soften but not completely cook. (Or you can boil the leaves, in which case save the water to use later to dilute the cooking sauce.)
- Rinse the cabbage in cold water.
- Separate the 12 largest leaves, and mop them dry with absorbent paper. (Use the rest of the cabbage as a vegetable for another meal).
- Mix the minced meat, onion, breadcrumbs, tomato paste, parsley, herbs and seasoning in a bowl.
- Arrange a cabbage leaf in front of you with the stem pointing towards you.
- Place a spoonful of stuffing in the middle, and roll the base forward to cover it.
- Fold the sides up and continue rolling forward, sealing the package like an envelope.
- Spear with a toothpick, or tie with string.
- Pack the 12 cabbage packets into a wide saucepan (or you can pack them together firmly without tying and they won't come undone).
- Heat the chopped tomatoes, brown sugar and lemon juice in a pan, and pour over the cabbage, adding enough water to cover.
- Cook, uncovered, on the top of the stove on a very low heat for 2 hours, adding a little boiling water from time to time if it starts to dry out.

GERMANY

Glazed Turnips

This rural old-fashioned recipe from Silesia in southern Germany enhances the vegetable's nutty sweetness. It goes very well with a pork dish, in which case, use pork stock for the turnips.

SERVES 4

1½ lb turnips, washed, peeled and cut in half
2 fl oz olive oil (or butter)
1½ pints good beef, chicken or pork stock
1 tablespoon flour
1 tablespoon sugar
salt and pepper
sprig of parsley, finely chopped, to garnish

- In a large frying pan (preferably non-stick) heat the oil (or butter), add the sugar and stir continuously with a wooden spoon until the mixture becomes a light-brown caramel.
- Add the turnips and brown gently for about 5 minutes, tossing, to prevent sticking.
- Add enough stock to half cover the vegetables, and simmer gently for about 15 minutes.
- Mix the flour to a paste with a little of the remaining stock and add to the sauce to thicken it slightly.
- Cook for a few minutes more, stirring constantly, and season to taste with salt and pepper.

BELGIUM

Ardennes Carrots

At one level the Belgians eat the most sophisticated food in Europe, the best equalling anything in France's top restaurants; on another, they have a long-standing country tradition of good peasant food, and this treatment raises a winter carrot to kingly status. This dish also employs to advantage their excellent cured ham and calls for the best that can be obtained. It might be served as a side-dish, with a plate of boiled beef (*boeuf bouilli*) and is a variation, therefore, of our boiled beef and carrots.

SERVES 4

1 lb winter carrots, cut into strips
1 lb onions, finely sliced
4 oz smoked bacon or cured ham, such as Ardennes (or Parma)
2 oz olive oil (or pork fat)
½ tablespoon flour
pinch sugar
sprig parsley, chopped
salt

- Fry the ham or cured bacon slowly in the oil (or lard) with the onions.
- Sprinkle with flour, stirring continuously, and when the flour begins to colour, blend in ½ pint warm water, stirring all the time.
- Add the carrots and cook slowly, uncovered, with a little salt and sugar for about 45 minutes to 1 hour, allowing as much water as possible to evaporate.
- Serve garnished with parsley.

INDIA

Spiced Cauliflower and Potato

Cauliflower, like cabbage, benefits from a short cooking time, to keep its juicy, crunchy texture. Spiced, as it is in this dish, it assumes a new distinction, and the potatoes give a contrast in texture. If you have cold cooked potatoes in the fridge it is an extremely quick dish too. I have been cooking it ever since I saw Maddhur Jaffrey demonstrate it on television.

SERVES 2

1 small cauliflower, stripped of leaves, cut into florets
½ lb cooked potatoes, cut into ¾ inch pieces
1 green chilli, deseeded (or not) finely chopped
½ teaspoon whole cumin seeds
*2 teaspoons good curry powder, preferably home-made**
salt and pepper, cayenne pepper
cooking oil (sunflower or ground nut)

- Heat some oil in a pan over medium heat. Put in the whole cumin seeds and cook for a few seconds till they sizzle and pop.
- Add the cauliflower florets and cook for 2 minutes, letting them brown a bit.
- Stir in the curry spices and cook for 2 minutes more, stirring well.
- Add a cupful of water. Put a cover on the pan and cook for another 5 minutes till nearly done.
- Add the potato, mixing gently with a spoon.
- Cook with the lid off for 3 minutes or so, till the potatoes are heated through.
- Season with salt, pepper and cayenne pepper.

Freshly ground spices

- In a dry frying pan, heat 1 teaspoon whole cumin seed 1 teaspoon coriander seeds and ½ teaspoon fenugreek seeds till they start to give off their aromas.
- Grind in a coffee grinder or a mortar.
- Add ½ teaspoon each of turmeric and ginger powder.
- It's best made freshly, but can be kept in a small, airtight jar.

PHILIPPINES

Sweetcorn and Shrimp Fritters

These patties are delicious, with the young sweetcorn a juicy, sweet, crunchy contrast to the soft, salty meat of the prawns. A light summer dish served with rice.

SERVES 4

½ lb sweetcorn, stripped from about 4 cobs with a sharp knife (or ½ lb drained, canned sweetcorn)
½ lb shelled prawns, finely chopped
1 onion, finely chopped
2 cloves garlic, crushed, finely chopped
2 spring onions, chopped
2 tablespoons cornflour
2 tablespoons water
1 egg, beaten
salt and pepper
oil for deep frying

- Combine the sweetcorn with the prawns, garlic, onion, salt, pepper and sugar.
- Mix the cornflour to a smooth paste with the water, then combine it with the egg. Stir into the corn mixture.
- Pour oil into a frying pan to a depth of ¼ inch and heat it until a haze rises.
- Put in spoonfuls of the mixture, a few at a time, and fry until crispy golden brown on both sides.
- Drain the fritters on absorbent paper.

USA

Cauliflower and Sesame Quiche

This is a recipe from the New Wave school of vegetarians in America, embracing European cauliflower, Japanese sesame seed and spicy, filling, wholesome, whole-wheat pastry. It provides a happy combination of flavours: the hot, mustardy, savoury character of onion, cauliflower and cheese, balanced by the nutty sweetness of sesame seeds and milk.

SERVES 4

4 oz pastry, preferably wholewheat (see next page)
1 lb cauliflower, tough stalk removed
2 tablespoons sesame seeds
4 oz cheddar cheese
3 eggs
10 fl oz milk
6 spring onions, chopped
1 teaspoon dried thyme
salt and pepper
1 tablespoon groundnut oil

- Toast the sesame seeds till lightly brown in a frying pan without fat and set aside.
- In the same pan, heat the oil and fry the cauliflower florets until almost tender, adding a little water to prevent burning.
- Add pepper, salt, thyme and spring onions, and cook for a few more minutes. Off the heat, stir in the sesame seeds.
- Roll out the pastry to fill a quiche tin, sprinkle with half the grated cheese and cover with the cauliflower mixture, topping with the rest of the cheese.
- Beat the eggs and milk together, season and pour over the quiche.
- Cook in an oven preheated to 350°F, 180°C, gas mark 4 for 30 to 40 minutes.

WHOLEWHEAT PASTRY

4 oz wholewheat pastry flour	*3 oz butter*
pinch salt	*3 tablespoons cold water*

- Mix the salt into the flour, cut the butter into pea-sized pieces, and gently work them into the flour, till you can form it into a ball that sticks together, using the least possible water.
- Wrap it and leave it in the fridge to cool for half an hour, then roll out to the size of your pie or flan dish.

IRELAND

Colcannon

The Irish combine cabbage and potato and they call it colcannon. It is made with mashed potato and cooked cabbage mixed into a purée with milk or cream in which onions or leeks have been cooked.

SERVES 4

1 lb potatoes, boiled in their skins, mashed	*1 onion (or leek) chopped*
½ cabbage, outer leaves discarded	*½ pint milk*
	salt and pepper
	butter

- Simmer the onion (or leek) in milk with a knob of butter for 20 minutes, till soft.
- Boil the cabbage until tender, drain, and chop finely.
- Combine the cabbage, potato, onion and milk, seasoning with salt and pepper and adding a little more butter if necessary for
- It's traditionally served very hot, piled in a mound, but it's no longer nutritionally correct to suggest the traditional presentation – hot bacon fat dribbled into an indentation made in the top.

GERMANY

Potato Salad

Kartoffelsalat

Potato salad is one of the most universal dishes in Germany and like their excellent bread, it acts as a carbohydrate counterweight to the high fat in the diet due to eating a great deal of pork, and an even greater volume of superbly-manufactured Wurst (sausages). This is a less fatty version – in the north they mix in mayonnaise, which certainly makes it that much more sensuous. To make it into a more substantial dish, you can add chopped, hard-boiled eggs. Prepare the salad at least an hour in advance.

SERVES 4

2 lb waxy, firm potatoes
4 tablespoons white wine vinegar
2 tablespoons water
2 tablespoons sunflower or groundnut oil
2 teaspoons mild mustard
1 tablespoon finely chopped onion
2 teaspoons sugar
6 oz pickled gherkins, diced

- Boil the potatoes in their skins for 25 minutes, then drain and peel off the skins.
- Meanwhile combine the other ingredients, mixing thoroughly.
- Cut the potatoes into thin slices, and while they are still warm toss them in the dressing.
- Leave to stand for at least 1 hour.

SPAIN

Patatas Bravas

Brava means 'fierce', in this sense, fiercely hot. It's extraordinary that something so very simple can be so sensational: it may be the combination of two different kinds of hot sensation – the steaming hot potato and the keenly-hot chilli pepper spicing, sharpened and sweetened by the smooth tomato sauce. It is often found as an appetiser in Spanish tapas bars, where tomato sauce is heated with fried cubes of potato. This version uses less fat and is baked in the oven. There would often be prepared tomato sauce and precooked potatoes in the fridge in a Spanish home, in which case this is a very speedy dish.

SERVES 4

2 lb potatoes, par-boiled in their skins (about 15 minutes)
1 lb tomatoes (or 14 oz can tomatoes)
1 onion, finely chopped
2 cloves garlic, crushed
2 teaspoons tomato paste
3 small, dried red chillies, crumbled (or 1 teaspoon chilli powder)
salt
olive oil

- Make a tomato sauce, frying the onions in a little olive oil till soft but not brown. Add the garlic toward the end of cooking.
- Chop the tomatoes and add to the onions with tomato paste, and crumbled chillies (or chilli pepper) and simmer gently for 20 minutes, allowing the mixture to thicken slightly.
- Peel the potatoes, cut into ½ inch cubes, season, and add to the tomato sauce.
- When heated through, transfer the mixture to an oven dish and bake at 400°F, 200°C, gas mark 6, for 20 minutes or until tender.

SWITZERLAND

Rösti

Fried potatoes aren't on the agenda in the modern diet, but if you're going to have them you might as well do it in style with this classic dish, where in fact the proportion of fat to carbohydrate is not excessive. It's not a slimmer's dish, but on the other hand it's very nutritious. A simpler, less luxurious version, is made with cold, half-cooked potatoes, boiled in their skins the previous day, grated, patted into a cake and fried in fat in a pan till golden.

SERVES 4

1½ lb raw potatoes, peeled and grated
4 oz Emmenthal or Gruyère cheese, grated
2 tablespoons sunflower or groundnut oil (or butter)
salt

- Heat the oil (or butter) in a large, heavy frying pan.
- Sprinkle the grated potato with salt.
- Pile into the pan and fry for about 20 minutes, turning occasionally.
- Half-way through cooking, add the cheese.
- When the potatoes are tender, turn the Rösti on to a warm plate and serve immediately.

PAKISTAN

Potato Patties

Tiki

These traditional, flat, round cakes, known as *tiki* in India and Pakistan, are served at teatime with a cup of tea. Mothers eat them all day long. A recipe for garam masala is given on page 250.

MAKES ABOUT A DOZEN

1 lb potatoes
dessertspoon garam masala
pinch chilli powder (to taste)
1 green chilli pepper, deseeded and chopped finely
fresh coriander leaves
pinch salt

For frying
1 egg
vegetable oil

- Wash the potatoes and boil in their skins till soft.
- Peel and mash them well, adding the garam masala, chilli powder, chilli pepper and salt.
- Mix with your hands, and make round, flat cakes (tikis).
- Beat the egg in a shallow dish.
- Heat a shallow layer of oil in a pan, and when hot, dip the tikis in the egg mixture, and fry in batches, turning to cook each side a golden brown.
- Drain on kitchen paper.

IRELAND

Boxty

This is as Irish a bread as a bread can be – potatoes combined with potatoes. The scones are divided into four 'farls'. My mother used to make this for me for tea if there was any left-over cooked potato in the pantry (before the days of the fridge). Left-over boxty is fried for breakfast in Ireland.

MAKES 8 FARLS

1 lb potatoes, peeled
1 lb potatoes, boiled in skins, cooked
2 oz plain flour
1 teaspoon salt
1 teaspoon bicarbonate of soda

- Grate the raw potatoes, and squeeze out their liquid between your hands.
- Mash the boiled potatoes in a bowl and mix with the grated potato, flour, salt and bicarbonate of soda.
- With your hands pat out the dough in a circle on a floured board to a thickness of ½ inch.
- Cut into quarters and place on a greased baking sheet.
- Bake in a preheated oven at moderate heat, 350°F, 180°C, gas mark 4 for 35 minutes. Serve like scones, steaming hot, buttered.

BULGARIA

Baked Potatoes and Cheese
Kartofi Sus Sirene

This supper dish is eaten throughout Bulgaria. Use a dry cheese like Cheshire, white Stilton, or salty Greek Feta cheese to approximate the Bulgarian *Sirene* cheese. Serve with a green salad. It has a delicious golden crust when cooked.

SERVES 4 TO 6

2 lb large potatoes, peeled and sliced thinly
½ lb cheese crumbled, or grated
4 oz softened butter
pepper
3 eggs
generous ½ pint plain yoghurt

- Arrange about a third of the potatoes over the bottom of a deep, buttered, baking dish.
- Beat the cheese and butter together until smooth and spread half the mixture over the potatoes.
- Sprinkle with pepper, then repeat these layers and arrange the remaining potatoes on top. Dot with butter.
- Bake in a preheated oven at 350°F, 180°C, gas mark 4, for about 30 minutes or until the potatoes are softening.
- Beat the eggs and yoghurt together to make a smooth mixture and pour it over the potatoes.
- Bake for a further 30 minutes to set the egg mixture and brown the top lightly.

HUNGARY

Paprika Potatoes
Paprikás Burgonya

The secret of Hungarian cooking is the use of the spice paprika, made from different grades of red peppers: the best are graded 'noble'. There are two main categories: hot and mild. Paprika from any other country, such as Spain, does not bear comparison. Paprika is a thickening agent, as well as being a flavouring. Traditionally the cooking medium in Hungary is cured white pork fat, called *speck*. As a luxury dish, sour cream rather than tomato juice might be used. (Add the cream off the heat.)

SERVES 4

2 lb potatoes, peeled and cut into thick slices or quarters
1 medium-sized onion, finely chopped
3 tablespoons olive oil (authentically, use speck)
¼ pint tomato juice
1 clove garlic
1 teaspoon caraway seeds
2 teaspoons mild paprika
salt and pepper

- Fry the onion in oil (or speck) till soft and transparent.
- Add the paprika, salt and pepper, mix thoroughly and cook for a few minutes.
- Stir in the tomato juice.
- Crush the garlic, caraway seeds and salt together, and stir into the pan.
- Add the potatoes, cover the pan and cook over a very low heat until the potatoes are tender, 30–45 minutes, turning the potatoes carefully from time to time to prevent browning.
- Tomato juice may be used instead of cream, and garlic and caraway seeds may also be added.

ENGLAND

Bubble and Squeak

If fried foods are frowned on these days, there have to be exceptions, and this is one of them, a classic of the traditional north of England stove. It is cheap, of course, and quick, since you should be using yesterday's potatoes, which have been cooked in their skins, peeled and mashed with very little milk and a spoonful of olive oil (all right, butter).

SERVES 4

1 lb mashed potatoes
¼ Savoy cabbage, shredded
1 onion, finely chopped
1 teaspoon mustard
salt and pepper
2 tablespoons olive oil, for frying

- In a bowl blend the potatoes, cabbage, onion, mustard, salt and pepper.
- Heat 1 tablespoon of the oil in a wide frying pan (preferably non-stick) and spread the potato mixture on the surface with a palette knife or the back of a spoon.
- Fry on a medium heat for 5 minutes or until the bottom is a crisp brown.
- Cover with a large plate, holding with a tea cloth and carefully invert the 'cake' on to the plate.
- Heat another tablespoon of oil in the pan and slide the cake back in, the crisp side uppermost.
- The potato bubbles and the cabbage squeaks, and in 5 minutes it's ready to serve.
- Serve with boiled bacon, gammon or liver and bacon.

SWEDEN

Jansson's Temptation

One of Sweden's most famous dishes, 'a fish pie' with a difference. Some people hate salted fish served warm, but I love this dish. In Sweden they use pickled smelts, preserved in salt, spice and sugar, and they are better for the dish if obtainable. Jansson's Temptation is often served as part of a *smörgåsbord*, the Swedish feast-day table of a series of dishes, hot and cold. Careful eaters may choose to use slightly less cream or even experiment with lower fat alternatives.

SERVES 6

16 anchovy fillets (or pickled smelts)
6 medium potatoes, cut into matchsticks
3 medium onions, thinly sliced
1 tablespoon vegetable oil (or use oil from anchovies)
2 oz butter
about ⅓ pint cream
white pepper
sprig chopped parsley, to garnish

- Heat half the butter with the oil in a frying pan and cook the onion rings gently until they are soft and transparent, but do not let them brown.
- Butter an oblong fireproof dish, place a layer of potatoes in the bottom, then a layer of onions, then anchovies and finally a layer of potatoes. Sprinkle each layer with a little white pepper.
- Pour half the cream over the top, dot with butter and bake in the oven at 425°F, 220°C, gas mark 7, until the potatoes are golden brown on top.

- Add the remaining cream and continue to bake until the potatoes are tender and the liquid has been absorbed (about 45 minutes).
- Sprinkle with chopped parsley and serve piping hot.

GERMANY

Heaven and Earth
Himmel und Erde

From the south of Germany, a country meal which makes a substantial but simple lunch with country or wholemeal bread and probably a glass of cold, German-brewed lager.

SERVES 4

2 lb potatoes
¾ lb cooking apples
1 oz sugar
2 onions, sliced
½ lb black pudding, sliced
2 tablespoons oil (or 1 oz butter)
salt, pepper, nutmeg

- Boil the potatoes in their skins.
- Peel, core and quarter the apples and stew in a little water with the sugar until soft.
- Drain and sieve; keep warm.
- Fry the onions in the oil (or butter); fry the sliced black pudding until crisp.
- Peel and mash the potatoes and while they are still hot, beat in the apple purée, salt, pepper and nutmeg, and a knob of butter to make it smooth.
- Serve the fried black pudding with the potato and apple purée, sprinkled with fried onion.

WEST INDIES

Baked Yam

Yams are the starchiest of all starchy vegetables. Crisp and white as snow inside, in contrast to the grey, hairy hippopotamus hide which encloses them. There are round ones like swedes, and long ones, the shape of ballooning carrots (there is also a yellow-fleshed variety). When cut open, they exude a slimy goo. Pop them straight into water, slightly acidulated with lemon juice or a teaspoon of vinegar.

SERVES 4

2 lb yam (two large ones)
4 tablespoons flour
1 teaspoon salt
freshly ground black pepper
2 oz fromage frais or butter
2 tablespoons milk

- In a bowl (or a paper bag) mix the flour, salt and pepper. Peel the yams, cut into quarters and dredge with flour (or shake in the bag).
- Bake on a metal grid at 400°F, 200°C, gas mark 4 for about 45 minutes, testing with a skewer for doneness.
- When they are soft inside, cut an incision in the toughened outer skin, remove the pulp with a spoon, and mash with fromage frais (or butter), milk, and salt and pepper.
- Return them to the oven to cook for 10 more minutes (or finish under the grill).
- Serve as a vegetable with a spicy meat or fish stew.
- You can also boil yams and finish them under the grill. Peel and quarter the yams, and boil in well-salted water for 20 minutes, or till tender. Leave till cool enough to handle, then slice, and grill, brushed with butter and sprinkled with salt and pepper.

WEST INDIES

Fried Plantains

The green 'bananas' in Caribbean shops are usually not bananas at all but plantains, suitable only for cooking, whether green, yellow, brown or black. They can be boiled but are best cut into chips and served as a vegetable like a potato. In the tropics it is no luxury but a cheap and convenient source of useful carbohydrate.

SERVES 4

2 large ripe plantains — *oil or butter for frying*

- Cut off both ends of the plantains and peel them. (Ripe plantains will usually peel as easily as ripe bananas, but if there is any difficulty, cut through the skins lengthways on the ridges with a small, sharp knife, then peel off the skin in sections.)
- Cut the plantains in half lengthways and crossways.
- Heat a thin layer of oil (or butter) in a large, heavy frying pan.
- Toss the pieces until browned on both sides, and then drain on kitchen paper. Serve immediately, while hot.

WEST INDIES

Baked Sweet Potato

Red-skinned sweet potatoes, with their sweet yellow flesh, can be cooked in the same way as yams to preserve their sweetness. In the Southern States of America sweet potatoes are sometimes boiled, sliced, and then candied in a frying pan with butter and sugar, to be served with a main course, such as salty gammon.

2

BEANS AND PULSES

If the world ran short of animal protein no one would suffer. Most of the essential amino acids (in protein) which are necessary for human growth are available in the world's family of beans and what amino acids are missing are supplied by the protein in bread. Thus baked beans on toast is the perfect complementary dish, providing the necessary nutrients as effectively as meat.

There are 18,000 genuine species of the *legume* family, seed bearing trees, shrubs and plants; the most successful are the common bean (*Phaseolus vulgaris*) of the Americas, the lentils (or *dal*) in India, the soya bean in the Orient, the pigeon pea in the Caribbean. They were well known in Europe too, providing the poor with sustenance before the arrival of the potato.

In Britain today a tin of beans is still the most popular canned vegetable, but we may be the only country in the world not to exploit the extraordinary potential of the dozens of kinds of beans and pulses, from tiny lentils to large fava beans. Beans are full of energy, vitamins and fibre. The one objection used against them, that they generate wind, can be reduced by careful cooking (rinsing away the water you soak them in, and the water you cook them in, before adding a tasty, rich sauce of your own) and also by eating them in modest quantities as part of a balanced meal, such as the beans and rice eaten in Latin America, and the lentils and rice eaten in India.

Guide to beans and pulses

Adzuki beans Like miniature red kidney beans. They are very pretty, prized in both China and Japan for their sweetness and delicacy, and often used in sweet dishes, made into a paste like chestnut purée. Boil the beans for 10 minutes, drain, and soak overnight. Cook for 1–1½ hours.

Black beans (Turtle beans or *frijoles negros*) Spectacularly beautiful, shiny, sleek beans prized in the Caribbean, Central America and Brazil. Eaten with rice, making a stark visual contrast, there is a dish known as 'Moors and Christians'. In Cuba they bathe the cooked beans in cider vinegar, chopped onions and red peppers, flavoured with cumin and oregano, and pour a hot tomato sauce on top. In Brazil they are the essential ingredient of the national dish, *feijoada*. Boil the beans for 10 minutes, and drain, before soaking overnight. Simmer for approximately 1½ hours.

Black-eyed beans (They are actually peas) Much used in the South of the United States where they were formerly a staple on the slave plantations. Earthy and chewy, they combine well with the metallic taste of spinach. Garlic gives them a lift. They need no pre-soaking. Cook for 20–30 minutes. Don't overcook as they go mushy.

Borlotti beans Pretty brown beans, speckled like thrushes' eggs, prized in Italy for vegetable soups, as they cook to a creamy delicacy. Often used in minestrone, or cooked with ham bones to provide a savoury backdrop. Parmesan cheese is a natural partner. Soak overnight. Boil for 1 hour or until tender.

Broad beans (Fava beans) White or brown. The skins are very tough and need to be removed after cooking, but it's possible to buy them already skinned, usually in Greek Cypriot shops. In Turkey they are boiled and served whole with an oil and vinegar dressing or cooked and puréed with oil, lemon and herbs to make an appetiser or dip. In Egypt, soaked, uncooked beans are puréed in a blender with herbs and spices to make a *falafel* mixture made into small cakes or patties and quickly fried. In Egypt there is a smaller type of brown broad bean known as *ful medames* which has an earthy, savoury, full flavour. Boil for 10 minutes, drain and discard the liquid, and soak overnight. Boil for 1½ hours approximately.

Butter beans (Also known as lima beans) Lovely, large, floury white beans with plenty of texture, and a nutty, mild flavour. In Jewish cooking they are combined with brisket of beef to make a delicious stew which is extremely nourishing and very inexpensive. They are traditionally served with fatty meats such as pork and goose, but also absorb delicious tomato sauces effectively. The first settlers to America were introduced to the native Indian recipe of *succotash*, a thick soup of cooked sweetcorn, butter beans and diced meat.

Cannellini (Also known as *fazolia* in Greece) Small white kidney beans used in salads and soup (*fasolada*) with a tender delicate flavour. Soak overnight, boil for 1½ hours approximately.

Chickpeas (*Garbanzos* in Spain, *ceci* in Italy, *channa* in India) Nutty, sweet and crunchy. An exciting ingredient in the best soups and stews of Spain, Italy and North Africa, not to mention the Middle East where it is the essential ingredient of both *hummus* dips, and the tasty fried snacks, *falafel*, especially in modern Israel. In India, chickpeas are prized as a vegetable dish in their own right. They need longer soaking and longer boiling than most pulses – some chefs soak them for no less than 48 hours. Allow 4 hours' simmering time (but some chickpeas actually take 6 hours). A pressure cooker shortens the time – but patience is the obvious solution. Just make sure you top up the pan with boiling water, more chickpeas burn dry than any other pulses.

Flageolets A tender, pale green (occasionally white) bean of the haricot family, more delicate in both flavour and texture, and pleasantly gooey. The French serve them traditionally with lamb dishes. They are very pretty combined with red kidney beans and white haricot beans as a three bean salad, with an oily, well-seasoned, mustardy vinaigrette dressing.

Haricot beans Also known as Boston navy bean and, as such, the principal ingredient in Boston baked beans, the forerunner of modern canned baked beans. The main difference is that the original was richly flavoured with pork and black molasses (treacle). The French make their rich *cassoulet* bean stew with haricot beans, lamb, pork, sausage and preserved goose. The Spanish use them in their famous *fabada asturiana,* the Basque stew of pork and *chorizo* sausage. The Italians, who call them *fagioli,* put them in *minestrone,* or serve them as a salad with tuna and herby dressing. The French serve them puréed with *gigot* (leg) of lamb, mixed with garlic, tomato sauce and some juices from the roast.

Lentils Lentils are enjoying an important revival in fashionable restaurants. The most fashionable are the stony, grey-green *lentilles de puy,* which keep their lens-like shape when cooked. They lend themselves to spicy, olive oil-based dressings and dishes where they soak up meat juices. The lens (of the eye) was named after the prized Roman pulse, not the other way round. Lentils have a meaty, savoury flavour and give body and substance to soups and stews. Along with rice, they form the staple food of the subcontinent of India where they are known as *dal.* They come in every colour of the spectrum – red, orange, yellow, green, brown, blue, mauve, beige and pink. They vary in size and texture, and in some Indian dishes are combined. Although they lack positive flavour, they combine well with spices.

Split lentils Yellow, orange or red. These are pulses with the skin removed and cook quickly, often to a pulp. Make them into a purée, after simmering with onion and garlic.

Lentils need no prior soaking. Whole lentils cook in 30–40 minutes, split lentils in 20–30 minutes.

Mung (or moong) beans (Also called green gram) This is the bean that is sprouted to make the Chinese vegetable, bean sprouts. All seeds and beans can be sprouted, but the mung bean gives the most succulent, juicy result for mixing into a stir-fry. Apart from giving added texture, the bean sprout is nature's power pack, delivering vitamins and minerals to the consumer in an edible raw form. You can also combine them with salad ingredients. The mung bean is known as green gram in India, where it is used like a lentil, or milled into flour for making cakes and butters.

Peanuts These are not in fact nuts at all, but pulses. The seeds grow in pods under the soil (hence groundnuts). High in oil content, a staple ingredient of African stews, contributing in South East Asia to delicious sweet and savoury dressings for salads and sauces for *satay* sticks (skewered pieces of marinated beef, pork and chicken).

Peas Split green peas and split yellow peas. The Swedish make a traditional yellow split pea soup with salt bacon, onions, cloves and ginger. They are also part of an old English tradition, and at one time it was daily cottage fare, made into a slab of pease pudding. 'Pease pudding hot, pease pudding cold, pease pudding in a pot, nine days old'. The peas are cooked with a ham bone or salty bacon, onion and herbs for several hours. Eat it with pork, bacon or ham, as a lump, or thinned into a purée, or make it into a thick soup. The Dutch make green pea soup with smoked sausage or frankfurters. You can buy tins of pease pudding very cheaply. It's very good value.

Pigeon pea (Gunga beans in the South of the United States, yellow *dal* in India). In the Caribbean, the traditional dish of 'rice and peas' uses pigeon peas, either fresh or dried. Rather an assertive, strong flavour.

Pinto beans Pinto means speckled, and these beans are like the pretty borlotti beans and should be used in the same way. Common in the United States.

Red kidney beans Probably the best-looking bean of all, with a shiny, mahogany brown sculptural form. The essential bean in Mexican cooking and the heart beat of a *chilli con carne*. This is the bean of *refritos*, the cooked beans being crushed and fried with oil and slices of sausage, and sometimes served with grated, sharp cheese. In Spain they are served with tomato sauce and rice as a main course, in Italy, in soups. In Greece and America the cooked beans are added to a three-bean salad with a mustardy, garlicky, oily vinaigrette dressing. Boil for 10 minutes, discard water, and soak overnight. Cook for 1½ hours.

Rosecoco A pretty pink bean enjoyed in the Caribbean and Latin America.

Soya beans The world's most versatile bean, providing an excellent oil (soya oil is highly prized in the food industry). A flour is milled from the bean and mixed with water to make a protein-rich milk, from which is made bean curd, also a protein food. The curd in turn can be salted and fermented to make *tempeh*, a savoury curd. The soy bean is also fermented and salted to make yellow bean sauce (used in Chinese cooking) and black beans (a salty savoury accompaniment to stir-fry dishes). The mashed, fermented, matured beans also make soy sauce.

The soya bean was also the guinea-pig in the making of meat analogues, and in St Louis, Georgia, heart of the United States bean belt, scientists developed TVP (textured vegetable protein) turning the processed bean into extrudable material which was woven in muscle patterns of beef, lamb, pork and chicken. But in Britain TVP chunks have been overtaken by Quorn which is made from a woven fungus of the mushroom family.

Soya beans are smaller than haricot beans, but lend themselves to similar treatments, and are excellent baked with a sauce, holding their texture while absorbing juices and flavours. Soak overnight, then simmer for about 1½ hours, drain, mix with a spicy tomato or meaty sauce and bake in a moderate oven for 30–40 minutes.

Soy beans prepared in the same way as mung beans are also excellent for sprouting.

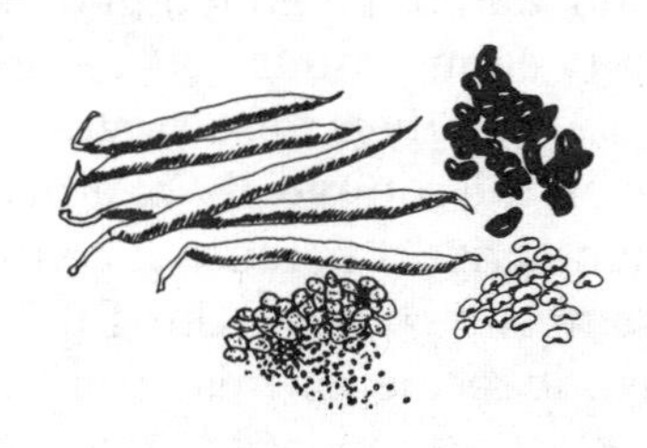

JAPAN

Miso Soup

Miso is a rich savoury, meaty paste made from fermented soya beans and rice. Its depth of flavour makes Western yeast pastes, which it partly resembles, seem crude in comparison, and in Japan it's understood to be part and parcel of healthy eating. Gourmets are extremely particular about choosing their miso pastes, some of which are aged, and take on the complexity of a mature cheese, for example. Vegetarians prize it because it contains a balance of amino-acids (protein) sometimes lacking in their diet.

This is the authentic recipe for miso soup which is the most popular breakfast dish in Japan. It is still possible to make an excellent soup with it, say for a first course at lunch, or for supper, without using seaweed (*wakame*) or even tofu. But the dried bonito shavings (*katsuobushi*) give it an essential character. Alternatively, use the miso as an extra savoury ingredient to add interest to a vegetable soup which has turned out to be on the thin side.

SERVES 4

2 tablespoons aka miso (red soya bean paste) or 2½ tablespoons milder shiro miso (white soya bean paste)
4–6 oz tofu (Japanese bean curd) cut into cubes
2 inch piece of kombu (kelp)
½ teaspoon wakame seaweed
2 teaspoons katsuobushi shavings (dried bonito)
2 pints water

- Put the kombu in a bowl with the water and leave to stand for 2–3 hours.
- Shortly before preparing the soup, put the wakame to soften in a little water for not more than 10 minutes, then cut it into small pieces.
- Put the kombu and its water in a pan over a medium heat. Just before the water comes to the boil, remove and discard the kombu.
- Add the bonito shavings, bring back to the boil, simmer for 2–3 minutes and remove the pan from the heat.
- Leave to stand for 4–5 minutes, until the bonito shavings have sunk to the bottom.
- Pour off the clear liquid and add a few tablespoons of it to the soya bean paste.
- Stir until smooth, then stir back into the soup and bring to the boil.
- Add the wakame and tofu, heat through and serve immediately.

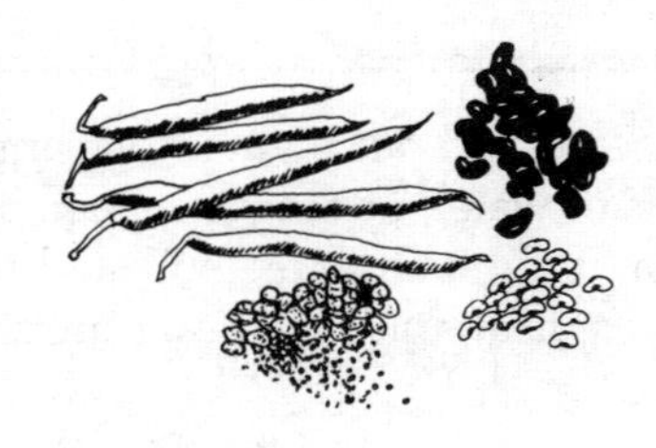

USA

Black Bean Soup

Beans were among the first staples of the American colonists and this smooth, nourishing soup lives on, a favourite everywhere.

SERVES 4

½ lb black beans, soaked overnight
½ lb stewing steak or veal (and preferably some of the bones)
1 large onion, chopped
2 teaspoons salt
pinch allspice
2 cloves
½ lemon, sliced
1 glass sherry

- Drain the black beans and put them into a large saucepan. Cover them with 3 pints of water, adding the meat, bones, onion, salt, spices and lemon. Bring it all to the boil, and simmer for 4 or 5 hours on the lowest heat, until the beans are starting to fall apart.
- Remove the bones and meat and tear the latter into shreds. Reserve. Discard the lemon and the cloves.
- Put the beans through your blender in batches, a small amount at a time, with enough water to process them until smooth. This can be done in advance if you prefer, and the bean purée kept in the fridge.
- To finish, heat the mixture, adding the sherry and a little more liquid if necessary, and simmer for a further 5 minutes.
- Serve the black bean soup in bowls garnished with more lemon slices.

SAUDIA ARABIA

Red Lentil Soup with Rice

In many Muslim countries this soup made with red lentils is eaten throughout the fast of Ramadan. Red lentils cook to a pulp after about 40 minutes so they are ideal for soups. Lentils are a good source of protein, so this makes a nourishing and appetising winter dish.

SERVES 4

8 oz red lentils, carefully picked over
2 tablespoons oil
1 large onion, chopped
1 clove garlic, peeled and crushed
1¾ pints chicken (or other) stock
salt and pepper
½ teaspoon ground coriander
½ teaspoon cumin
juice ½ lemon
3 tablespoons rice

- Heat the oil in a large saucepan and fry the onion in it until lightly coloured.
- Add the garlic and stir until golden.
- Stir in the lentils and pour on the stock.
- Season with salt and pepper and add the coriander, cumin and lemon juice.
- Bring to the boil and simmer gently until the lentils break up (about 40 minutes).
- Add the rice, and more water if the consistency is too thick. Simmer until the rice is tender.

USA

Split Pea Soup

This American soup has its origins in Europe, combining split peas and pearl barley. It is warming, easy to make and inexpensive. It's convenient too if you make a batch for warming up on another day. Keep it in a bowl in the fridge, covered with cling film.

SERVES 6 TO 8

1 lb split green peas, soaked
3 oz pearl barley
4 pints water
2 teaspoons sea-salt
2 bay leaves
2 tablespoons olive oil
1 medium onion, chopped finely
1 carrot, chopped finely
2 cloves garlic, peeled and crushed
2 teaspoons chopped fresh thyme (or 1 teaspoon dried thyme)

- Put the peas and barley in a large, heavy-based pan with the water, salt and bay leaves. Bring to the boil, then reduce the heat, cover and simmer for about 1 hour, stirring occasionally to prevent sticking.
- Heat the oil in a frying pan and sauté the onion, carrot, garlic and thyme in it until the carrot is tender.
- Add to the peas and barley and simmer for at least 30 minutes more.
- Remove the bay leaves and adjust the seasoning, adding more salt if necessary.

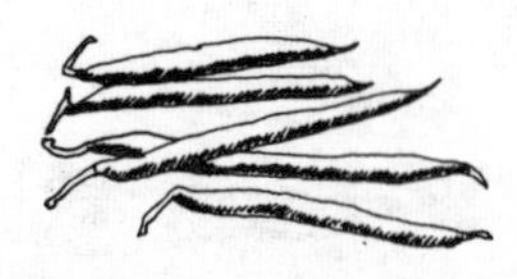

GREECE

Hummus

This has become one of the most popular summer dips in Britain. It's not necessary to buy it in supermarkets from the chill displays when you can make it to your own taste using a tin of chickpeas and thinning them, adding oil, lemon, garlic and parsley to taste – and of course *tahina*, the paste of crushed, toasted sesame seeds which can be bought in jars in Cypriot shops. It's satisfying to make your own from dry chickpeas and of course, a great deal cheaper. Buy chickpeas from a store with a rapid turnover, like Asian shops (Indians use *channi* – chickpeas – in their cooking all the time). If cooking with chickpeas, think ahead to allow the longest possible soaking, at least overnight.

SERVES 4

8 oz chickpeas
2 tablespoons tahina paste (sesame meal)
juice 2 lemons
2–3 cloves garlic, peeled and crushed
salt and pepper

For the garnish
parsley
cayenne pepper or paprika
black olives

- Put the chickpeas to soak in cold water overnight.
- Drain and boil them in fresh water for about 3 hours.
- Drain but keep the cooking liquid and reserve a few chickpeas.
- Put the chickpeas into a blender with enough cooking liquid to make a thick cream.
- Add the tahina paste, lemon juice, garlic, salt and pepper to taste. Beat till smooth.
- Serve garnished with the parsley, cayenne pepper or paprika, black olives and some whole chickpeas.

ISRAEL

Falafel

These crunchy, nutty cakes made from pounded, soaked, chickpeas and fried in hot oil have become the street food of Israel where they are eaten as a stuffing for pitta bread with salad and a little savoury *tahina* (sesame seed paste). Falafel mixes can be bought in packets but are by no means as tasty or satisfying as the real thing.

SERVES 4

1 lb chickpeas
4 oz onion, grated
8 spring onions, finely chopped
2–3 cloves garlic, crushed
1 teaspoon ground cumin
2 teaspoons ground coriander
salt and pepper
bunch fresh coriander leaves (or flat-leafed parsley, finely chopped)
pinch cayenne or chilli pepper
oil for frying

- Chickpeas vary in age. Plan to soak them for 24 hours, or even 48 hours, covered in plenty of water. They should be reconstituted to a chewy, raw texture.
- Drain them well and put through a blender in batches, to make as smooth a paste as possible.
- In a bowl mix in the remaining ingredients. Leave to rest for half an hour at least before cooking.
- With your hands, make walnut-sized balls, and slightly flatten them on a board.
- Leave them to rest for another 15 minutes.
- Heat a shallow layer of oil in a frying pan till very hot, and fry them for about 3 minutes each side, until golden brown.

EGYPT

Falafel

The falafel originates from Egypt where it's believed it goes as far back as the Pharaohs. The Egyptians make theirs with skinned white beans (a kind of broad bean) which can be bought in Greek–Cypriot stores. This recipe is almost identical to the one on the previous page.

SERVES 4

1 lb white broad beans
4 oz onion, grated
8 spring onions, finely chopped
2–3 cloves garlic, crushed
1 teaspoon ground cumin
2 teaspoons ground coriander
salt and pepper
bunch fresh coriander leaves (or flat-leafed parsley, finely chopped)
pinch cayenne or chilli pepper
oil for frying

- White broad beans vary in age. Plan to soak them for 24 hours, or even 48 hours, covered in plenty of water. They should be reconstituted to a chewy, raw texture.
- Drain them well and put through a blender in batches, to make as smooth a paste as possible.
- In a bowl mix in the remaining ingredients. Leave to rest for half an hour at least before cooking.
- With your hands, make walnut-sized balls, and slightly flatten them on a board.
- Leave them to rest for another 15 minutes.
- Heat a shallow layer of oil in a frying pan till very hot, and fry them for about 3 minutes each side, until golden brown.

MALAYSIA

Bean Sprouts

Bean sprouts are added to hot and cold mixed dishes to give a crisp texture. Because they are germinated seeds they are also rich in vitamins B and C. All kinds of seeds can be sprouted (what else was the mustard and cress we grew on wet flannels, or on wet blotting paper in jars at school?). Sprouted seeds were an essential cornerstone of the macrobiotic way of life in the 1960s and 1970s. Chinese bean sprouts are made from mung beans usually available in whole food stores and Asian shops. You can also sprout fenugreek, soya beans, lentils, wheat and other grains satisfactorily. Add to salads, or Chinese stir-fry dishes.

MAKES A JAR FULL

about 2 oz mung beans for a 1 lb jar

- Put the mung beans in a large jam jar and fill it with cold water.
- Cover the top with a piece of muslin held on with a rubber band and leave the jar overnight with the water in.
- Next day pour off the water through the cloth and put the jar in a cool, dark place.
- Twice a day fill it with fresh cold water to rinse the seeds, and then pour off through a cloth. Soon they will begin to sprout. You can judge for yourself when they are ready, usually after 2 or 3 days.

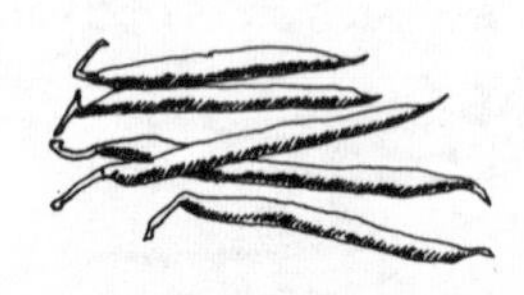

USA

Three Bean Salad

This is a colourful and appetising combination of red and white dried beans and fresh green beans which makes a delicious, easy, summer lunch. It even improves with keeping in the fridge for a second day when the flavours of the dressing soak in. It's an economical and practical dish, especially when you have cooked a surplus of beans for other meals.

SERVES 6

8 oz cooked red kidney beans (or a can)
8 oz cooked haricot or borlotti beans (or a can)
½ lb French beans (or runner beans)
8 oz pasta shells (or bows)
2 cloves garlic, crushed and chopped
4 tablespoons extra virgin olive oil
1 tablespoon white wine vinegar (or lemon juice)
1 teaspoon Dijon mustard
parsley or green coriander leaves
10 spring onions, chopped finely
1 teaspoon Dijon mustard
salt and pepper

- Boil the pasta in plenty of salted water till *al dente* (just slightly chewy) drain, and rinse in cold water.
- Cook the green beans in a little fast-boiling water, till slightly underdone.
- Drain, and refresh in cold water.
- Make a dressing with the oil, vinegar (or lemon juice), garlic, mustard, salt and pepper.
- Mix with the dry and green beans and spring onions.
- Sprinkle with the herbs and chill for an hour or two.

FRANCE

Haricots

Haricot beans make the classic *cassoulet* of Castelnaudary. These ingredients act like sponges, soaking up unctuous juices and fat from *confit* of goose or duck. In Normandy, haricot beans serve a similar function, mopping up the juices of delicate *pré-salé* lamb, bred on the salt marshes. Here is a classic recipe.

SERVES 4 (WITH LAMB)

½ lb dried haricot beans (soaked overnight)
1 onion
1 carrot
bouquet garni (green of leek, stick of celery, sprig each of thyme and parsley, bay leaf)
2 medium tomatoes
butter for frying
juice from roast lamb

- Drain the beans and cover them with twice their volume of water, adding the whole onion, carrot, celery stick and bouquet garni. Bring to the boil, cover, and simmer for 1½–2 hours, making sure the water doesn't boil away. The beans are done when they are soft inside, the skins still unbroken.
- Drain the beans, reserving the liquid.
- Discard the carrot, celery and bouquet garni, but keep the onion, chopping it and frying in a little butter, adding the tomatoes and stirring to a paste. Season.
- Add the beans, and mix well, thinning to a smooth consistency, with some of the cooking liquid from the beans. Dribble the meat juices on top just before serving.
- NB Haricot beans vary in both quality and age. The best and youngest cook the most quickly.

IRAQ

Ful Medames

In Iraq a bowl of these savoury, rich, dark beans is served at breakfast with pitta bread. Each person dresses their own bowl with oil, lemon, parsley, garlic, spring onions and freshly ground cumin seed, set out on the table. A thicker, soupier bowl of *ful medames* is achieved by cooking a tablespoon or two or red lentils, which break up in the cooking.

SERVES 4 TO 6 (WITH PITTA BREAD)

1 lb fava (dark broad) beans | *2 tablespoons red lentils*

- Boil the beans in a saucepan for 10 minutes.
- Discard the water, cover again and soak the beans overnight.
- Discard this water, cover with fresh, unsalted water, and cook for 2 hours or until tender (adding the red lentils if you want a thicker mixture). Add salt towards the end of the cooking. If you add it too soon, the beans harden.
- Serve with a garnish as above.
- In some Arab countries it is served with quartered, hard-boiled eggs.

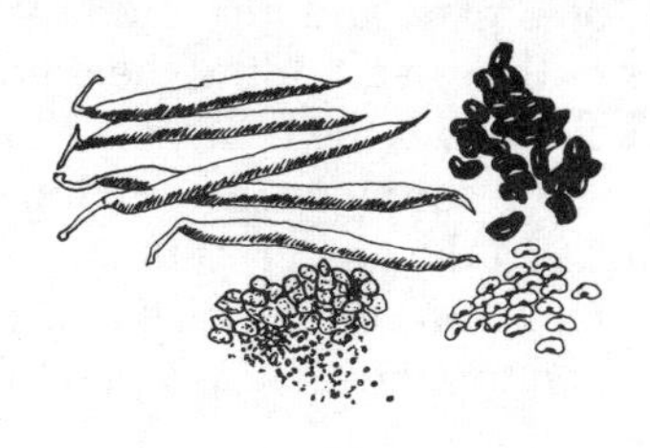

INDIA

Spicy Mixed Dal

The Indians live off *dal* (assorted lentils), rice and vegetables, and have infinite ways of spicing them to introduce variety. The tiny beans are brown, green, yellow, orange, bluey-grey and creamy-white, and each has a slightly different quality in the cooking. Some remain firm, others break up into a pulp. In this recipe five varieties are cooked together, giving the benefit of the qualities of each. In Asian stores you should find yellow lentils (*toovar* or *arhar dal*), pink (*masar dal*), green (*mung dal*), black and white (*urad dal* with and without skins) and yellow split peas (*channa dal*). You can blend as many of these kinds as you wish.

SERVES 4 (WITH BOILED RICE)

10 oz mixed lentils
1½ pints water
1 onion, chopped
1 teaspoon turmeric
1 green chilli, finely chopped
1 inch fresh ginger, grated
1 tablespoon garam masala
3 tablespoons vegetable oil
2 cloves garlic, finely sliced
2 teaspoons cumin seeds
coriander, mint or parsley garnish

- Spread the lentils on a plate and pick out any stones.
- Rinse well. Cover with water, adding the onion and turmeric, and bring to the boil. Lower the heat, cover and simmer for 35–45 minutes to a soft, soupy purée, stirring so it doesn't stick.
- When nearly done, add the ginger, chilli and garam masala.
- To serve, put the dal into a serving dish and pour sizzling, garlic-seasoned oil on top (heat oil in a pan to brown the garlic with the cumin seeds).
- Serve with rice or as a side dish with a curry meal.

IRAQ

Black-Eyed Beans and Spinach

Black-eyed beans are actually peas. They have a dull taste and a dry, chewy, texture, but this partnership with juicy, slippery spinach is a brilliant success, more than the sum of its parts. The leaves of Swiss chard can be used instead of spinach, but cut away the bitter stems. (The stems can be cooked till tender on their own, without leaves, in a cheese sauce, and served as a filling to a quiche or pastry tart.)

SERVES 4 AS A SIDE DISH, 2 AS A MAIN COURSE

6 oz black-eyed beans
1 lb fresh spinach (or 8 oz frozen leaf spinach, finely chopped)
1 large onion, finely chopped
4 tablespoons vegetable oil
salt and pepper

- You do not need to soak black-eyed beans. Cover them with water and boil for 20–30 minutes, checking for softness. Don't let them cook to a pulp. Add salt towards the end of cooking.
- Boil the spinach in very little salted water for 5 minutes.
- Drain in a sieve, pressing out surplus moisture.
- Fry the onion in hot oil till soft but not brown.
- Stir in the spinach, to heat through and add the black-eyed beans.
- Season to taste, and serve dressed with more oil.
- Eat with bread and perhaps a poached egg, or as a side dish.
- You can also serve it cold, as a first course in summer.

HOLLAND

Brown Beans with Apples

A rural winter dish from the apple growing areas of Holland where fruit is still dried by housewives for use in the winter. In Germany apples are cooked with potatoes to make Heaven and Earth (see page 71).

SERVES 6

¾ lb brown or red kidney beans
½ lb salt bacon or gammon, in 1 piece
6 oz dried apple, soaked overnight
1 tablespoon potato flour or cornflour

- Cover the soaked beans and apples with 1½ pints fresh water, add the piece of bacon, and simmer until they are tender (about 1½ hours).
- Drain off the liquid and thicken with the potato flour or cornflour to make a sauce.
- Slice the bacon, arrange it on top of the apples and beans, and pour the sauce over the top.
- Serve with boiled potatoes.

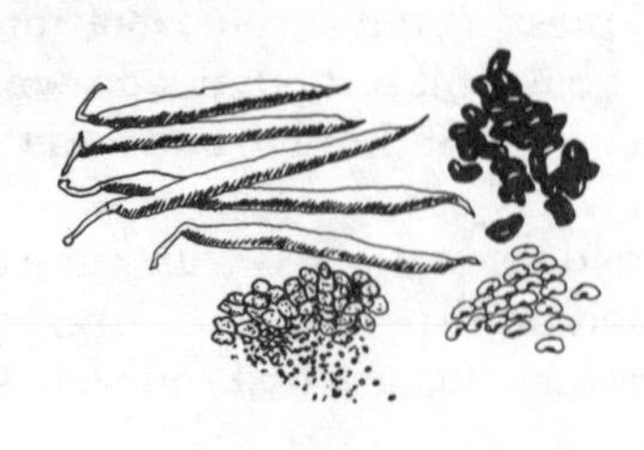

INDIA

Chickpeas and Potatoes
Channa Bhatora

Chickpeas are a staple food in the Punjab, and combined with potatoes are a frequent one-dish meal. Serve with a salad of raw sliced onion. Eat with Indian naan bread or Greek pitta bread.

SERVES 4 TO 6

1 lb chickpeas, soaked 24 hours, simmered till soft (or two 15 oz cans of chickpeas, drained)
12 oz potatoes, boiled in their skins (don't overcook)
½ lb tomatoes, skinned and chopped
4 teaspoons vegetable oil
1 teaspoon whole cumin seeds
1 teaspoon salt
1 teaspoon powdered turmeric
1 teaspoon fresh ginger, grated (or finely chopped)
2 teaspoons curry powder or garam masala
few drops lemon juice
¼ pint water
fresh coriander leaves

- Heat the oil in a frying pan, and toss in the cumin seeds, frying them till they pop.
- Add the tomato, and cook on a low heat for 10 minutes.
- Then add the salt, the rest of the spices and a squeeze of lemon and stir to form a thick sauce.
- Now add the chickpeas, potatoes and water, and simmer on the lowest heat for 15–20 minutes.
- After 10 minutes sprinkle with coriander leaves.

MEXICO

Casseroled Beans

Black beans, red beans, pinto beans and kidney beans are eaten every day in Mexico and Central America with great relish. Most families cook beans in large quantities to last several days, because not the least attractive dish is *frijoles refritos*, cooked beans fried up. Authentically, the beans are cooked with a herb called *epazote* which we don't have, but a bay leaf can be substituted. Make double quantities if you want to make *refritos*, the next recipe.

SERVES 4

8 oz dried beans (black, red, pinto, kidney)
½ lb onion, finely chopped
2 cloves garlic, crushed and chopped
2 chilli peppers (preferably serrano*) deseeded, chopped*
2 pints water (approximately)
2 tablespoons vegetable oil (or, authentically, lard)
salt

- Boil the dark-coloured beans in water for 10 minutes. Drain and soak in fresh water overnight.
- Drain again and put them in an oven casserole, with the onions, garlic, chillies, oil (or lard) and just cover with boiling water.
- Cook in a medium hot oven, 350°F, 180°C, gas mark 4, with a lid and cook until tender, 2 or 3 hours, adding a little boiling water if they start to dry out. (Or the beans can be cooked in a heavy, covered pan on the stove, simmering slowly.) Don't add the salt until towards the end of the cooking, or the beans will harden.
- For a thick sauce, when the beans are tender, remove a ladleful, mash, return them to the casserole and heat through.
- Adjust seasonings to taste.
- Serve with rice or tortillas.

MEXICO

Frijoles Refritos

Drained beans are fried in oil or lard, often with some chopped fried onion and sliced sausage (*chorizo*) and the beans mashed with the back of a spoon as they cook to make a purée. The dish is often served with crispy strips of fried tortilla (see recipe) and a *salsa cruda* (see recipe). It is served as an accompanying dish to a main course, as a filler.

SERVES 4

½–1 lb cooked beans (see previous recipe)

3 tablespoons vegetable oil (lard is authentic)

- Heat about 1 tablespoon oil (or lard) in a heavy frying pan or non-stick pan.
- Add 2 tablespoons beans and mash well over a high heat.
- Add more fat and more beans and continue mashing. Continue until you have finished the supply of beans and fat and have a coarse purée.
- They are ready to serve when the beans are hot and sizzling and crisp underneath.
- Eat with crispy fried strips of tortilla stuck into the beans and a bowlful of salsa cruda.

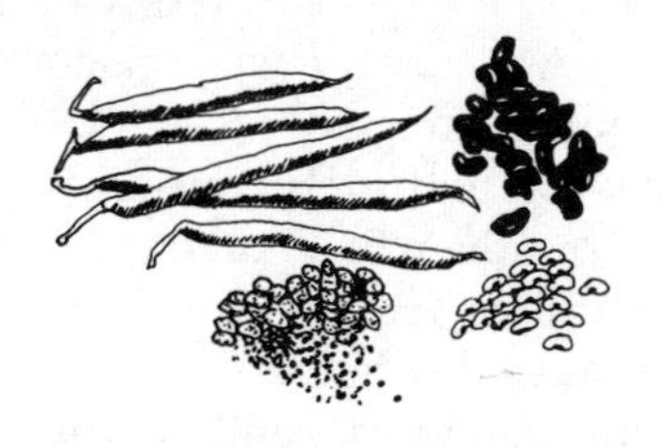

MEXICO

Chilli Con Carne

In Mexico this means beans with a little meat, spiced with hot chillies. In Texas it means beef (and sometimes pork) spiced with hot chilli (the hotter the better) and very few beans. It has grown into the most popular British pub dish (cheap to produce) and one of the few foods that can stand up to indifferent keg beer and fizzy cold lager and actually fight back. The worst examples taste of raw cayenne pepper. It is essential to fry the spices, and especially the cayenne or chilli pepper, for some minutes to 'temper' them before adding and simmering. Serve with boiled plain rice.

SERVES 4

1 lb red kidney beans
½ lb lean minced beef
½ lb onions
1–2 tablespoons sunflower oil
1–2 teaspoons chilli powder
2 cloves garlic
pinch cumin seed
1 teaspoon dried oregano or marjoram
½ teaspoon dried thyme
1 tin tomatoes
1 tablespoon tomato purée
about ¼ pint stock
salt and pepper

- First bring the beans to the boil covered with water, simmer for 10 minutes, then throw away the water as this contains toxins (all dark beans should be treated this way).
- Cover again with water and soak overnight.
- To cook the beans, put them in a pan of cold water, bring to the boil and simmer until just tender. (The time will vary according to the age of the beans – 1–2 hours.)
- Chop the onions finely, and fry gently in the sunflower oil until they are becoming translucent, then turn up the heat and add the mince.

- Stir it round, breaking it up with a wooden fork or spoon. When it is frying well, leave it alone so it can start to brown.
- Add the garlic, herbs and spices, and fry on.
- When the meat is browning nicely, add the tomatoes, tomato purée, seasoning and stock.
- Bring to simmering point, transfer the beans to the meat and keep their cooking liquid. As the bean and beef mixture becomes somewhat dry, add cooking liquid from the beans in small quantities to keep it just moist.
- Simmer for 1½ hours.

BRAZIL

Feijoada

The national dish of Brazil. If served *feijoada* in a rough café in São Paulo, you will rightly guess – as you dig out of the pot of gooey beans a gelatinous, salted, pig's tail, (unmistakably) the ear of a pig, and one of the animal's trotters – that the dish comes down from the slave plantations. However, in a private home, or smart restaurant, tremendous attention is paid to the shopping, preparation, cooking and presentation of a feijoada. The meats are taken from the stew carved, beautifully and arranged on a platter.

It is the black beans, so typical of South America, that give feijoada its authentic depth of colour and richness – but you can use red kidney beans. Note that before soaking you should fast-boil all dried beans for 10 minutes, then throw away the water, to remove the toxins.

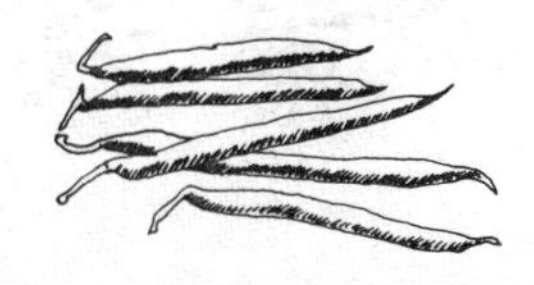

SERVES 6

1½ lb black beans (or red kidney beans) soaked for 12 hours
1 lb salt beef, also soaked for 12 hours
½ lb smoked pork (or knuckle of bacon)
1 pig's trotter (for texture)
½ lb cooking sausage (Spanish, Italian) cut into small pieces
1 onion, finely chopped
3 deseeded green chillies, finely chopped
2 cloves garlic, chopped
salt, pepper, olive oil

- Drain the beans and salt beef.
- Put the beef, pork (or bacon) and pig's trotter into a saucepan, cover with warm water, bring to the boil and simmer for 1½–2 hours, until they are tender.
- In another pan, cover the beans with water and cook for up to 2 hours, until they are soft enough to mash.
- Now combine the meat and beans, and cook them together gently to combine the flavours.
- In a frying pan, cook the onion in oil until it starts to colour.
- Add the cooking sausage, garlic and chilli, and heat through.
- Add a cupful of cooked beans and mash them in the pan with enough liquid to make a thick sauce. Season with salt and pepper.
- Cook for a few minutes, then stir into the meat and beans and cook till well blended.
- Serve with plain rice.
- A classic touch is to add a pint of fresh orange juice to the water in which the meat is simmered.

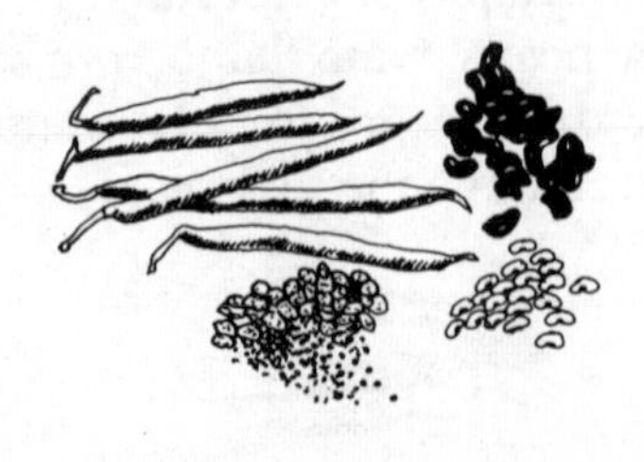

3

BREAD, PASTA AND PASTRY

Nothing in the world of food is quite as breathtaking as the making of bread. It is not just the alchemy which is marvellous enough, taking what is basically grass seed, pounding it, sieving it, and cooking it into extraordinary nourishing and appetising objects; you have that with pancakes and flatbreads and biscuits. What is really magical is the harnessing of armies of minute living organisms, living yeast cultures, and encouraging them to breed and multiply in the wet warmth of a ball of dough.

We can make dough rise by making gas by applying acid (sour milk, buttermilk, yoghurt, tartaric acid, lemon juice) to baking soda (bicarbonate of soda) mixing it with dough, and heating it. A soda bread (or scone) is a lovely soft mouthful, but it does not compare with the dough where the yeast cultures have been given time to mature and condition the dough.

The modern factory breadmaking process is fast, exceedingly fast. Extra yeast provides extra energy, and a 20 minutes spin in a mechanically accelerated dough mixer achieves a risen dough which used to take craft bakers all night to make. But what it gains in efficiency it loses in flavour and character. The marvel of breadmaking is the sourdough, a process by which the dough matures for days, even up to a week, to allow *lacto-bacilli* cultures to take over the work from yeast cultures, producing incomparable flavour, texture and keeping qualities.

But there is room for all kinds of bread, quick and slow breads, large and small, made with yeast and without, and not only with wheat flour, but maize, and barley, and oats and rye and buckwheat.

If the nutritional Pyramid suggests we should eat more bread, much, much more, let it be bread that is a feast in itself, not a tasteless sponge made in a factory, without feeling.

This section includes pancakes, flatbreads, pizza breads – and pasta, a subject in itself so enormous that it is almost insulting to touch on it so briefly. Pasta, eaten in the volume the Italians consume it, is a sure indicator of their excellent health status. It is also a happy coincidence that their cuisine is one of the finest in the world.

Nutritionists consider that Italy's high consumption of rice and pasta makes a considerable contribution to their excellent health record. Produced in a hundred different shapes, sizes, and even different qualities (freshly made soft pastas, factory-made dry pastas, and handmade thick, dry pasta) every meal, every day can be interestingly different. A dish of pasta provides the perfect Pyramid base of starch to some vegetables, meat or sauce on top, and at the top of the Pyramid, a little extra virgin cold-pressed olive oil, perhaps, or half an ounce of freshly grated, mature Parmesan cheese.

Guide to flours

WHEAT FLOUR

Wheat is the grain most used for baking bread; it gives the lightest, best-risen loaves. This is because it contains a substance called gluten which stretches and traps air bubbles during fermentation. Other grains have less gluten, or almost none at all, and make dense loaves with a marked taste compared to the blandness of bread made with plain white flour and preferred by many people. Wheat is milled to produce wholemeal flour or white flour.

WHITE FLOUR White flour is made by sieving wholemeal flour. The percentage of white flour extracted from the sieving is called the extraction rate. White flour sold in high street shops has an extraction rate of about 72%. That is to say 28% of fibre and bran has been removed.

Commercial white flour is made on roller mills. The bran and wheat germ are sifted out and the flour treated with a bleach to whiten and mature it. Some nutrients are lost in this process, but the government requires two B vitamins (thiamin and nicotinic acid) and some iron to be returned.

Self-raising flour White flour to which some baking powder has been added. Unfortunately you have no way of telling how old the flour is. The efficiency of baking powder deteriorates with time. Instead of self-raising flour, it is better to use plain flour and add your own baking powder.

Soft white flour From soft wheat, it has a low protein content which makes it ideal for making biscuits. Soft flour takes up less water and, apparently because of this, stales quickly. French *baguettes* are made with it and have a biscuity crust, but are quick-staling.

Strong white flour From hard wheat, it takes up more water and is best for bread you want to keep for more than a day.

Unbleached white flour This comes from the stoneground millers and consists of up to 80% extraction, which means that about 20% of the bran and wheat germ have been removed by sieving. Unbleached white flour has some traces of finely crushed wheat germ in it, which add to the flavour but, like wholemeal flour, will go off after about two months. It has a pleasing, creamy-yellowish colour. White loaves made with it will resemble bread eaten on holiday in Spain, Italy and the Balkans, and the French *pain de compagne*. If you can't buy it, you can make it youself by sieving wholemeal flour, to remove about one-fifth of the coarser material.

WHOLEMEAL FLOUR Wholemeal flour is also known as 100% wholewheat flour. This is made from the whole wheat grain, including the outside skin – the bran, as well as the wheat germ – the wheat berry's own tiny 'seed'. It has more flavour and contains more nutrients than white flour, particularly all the B vitamins, vitamin E, magnesium, potassium and iron. A well-balanced, modern, mixed diet should not be deficient in these nutrients but it is good that bread, being everyone's basic food, should provide them.

Wholemeal flour does not rise as well as white flour. The bran content makes it heavy and moist. The real problem with wholemeal is that it makes a heavy loaf. However, a little vitamin C powder (ascorbic acid) added to the dough mixture gives it a lift.

Wholemeal flour can be bought stoneground or ground by steel roller mills.

Stoneground This flour is the best-flavoured wholemeal, and is produced by crushing together the bran, wheat germ, and endosperm (which contains the bulk of the flour). Use as soon as possible, and do not keep for more than two months. After that, the oil in the wheat germ starts to go off, and gradually turns rancid. Store in a cool place. Stoneground flour keeps best refrigerated. Storing is not a problem if you mill your own wholemeal flour freshly at home from the whole grain, or buy small amounts regularly.

Steel roller milling The elements of the grain are separated and the bran and wheat germ are sieved away. This 'offal' usually goes for animal feed so farmers certainly recognise its tremendous nutritional value. The wheat germ is flattened, not broken, and heat-treated so that it will not go rancid. The process destroys some vitamins.

85% and 81% wholewheat flour This is a wholemeal flour which has had 15% to 19% of the coarser bran extracted, to make it lighter.

Brown flour (or wheatmeal) Wheatmeal is a misleading term because it is not what it sounds like, that is whole meal (whole wheat) flour, which includes the whole berry. Wheatmeal is really another name for brown flour. It is in fact white flour with a small quantity of finely milled bran returned to it.

Graham flour An American wholemeal flour which is coarsely milled and contains larger bran fragments. It is named after Dr Sylvester Graham, the food reformer, who was campaigning for wholemeal flour about a century ago.

Granary flour A proprietary brand of flour which includes some bran, some malt flakes and cracked wheat. It makes particularly nutty, well-flavoured bread and has sufficient gluten to make an attractive, well-risen loaf.

RYE FLOUR OR MEAL This greyish-brown flour, has a rich, slightly sweet flavour. It is usually combined with wheat flour to make solid breads, characteristic of Middle and Eastern Europe.

Rye contains less gluten than wheat so it makes a dense, moist loaf. The more rye flour added, the stickier the bread. A loaf entirely made with rye, like pumpernickel, produces a bread of a dark, pudding-like texture. A mixture of 50% rye and 50% unbleached white flour gives a good bread which slices thinly. The well-risen rye breads sold at bakeries contain around 80% white flour and 20%, or even less, rye flour. They do not usually have the special sour flavour which marks traditional rye bread. Because rye bread has very little gluten it requires less rising time than wheat flour, since the fermenting yeast meets less resistance.

Sourdough rye breads owe their flavour to lactic acid which is produced in the dough by the action of *lacto-bacilli.* To make a sourdough starter, mix equal weights of rye flour and warm water, for example 1 lb rye flour and 1 lb warm water, and leave covered in a warm place for two or three days. The mixture attracts micro-organisms such as *lacto-bacilli*, in the air. The yeast starts the fermentation process but soon the *lacto-bacilli* takes over, producing lactic acid and giving the paste a pleasant sour smell, like apple. The lactic acid inhibits undesirable micro-organisms which could turn the dough mouldy.

BARLEY FLOUR (OR MEAL) A small quantity combined with wheat flour, gives a slightly sweet and nutty flavour with a cake-like quality. Warm the dry flour before making the dough. Barley flour on its own has a low gluten content, and the loaf won't rise.

PEARL BARLEY The whole grain which has been soaked in water to soften the tough husks. These are then rubbed off. It is usually used to thicken soups, but it can be milled at home to make barley flour.

OATS The only grain which grows well in Scotland and forms the basis of its national dishes, porridge and oat cakes.

OATMEAL The de-husked grain is milled into a variety of textures, coarse, medium and fine. Real Scottish porridge is made with oatmeal rather than rolled oats. Use oatmeal in parkins, scones and oatcakes. An ounce or two of oatmeal adds texture to a bread dough.

CORNMEAL OR MAIZE FLOUR Cornmeal is made from the roughly milled grain of maize (dried corn-on-the-cob). It comes in various textures and can be added to make dough crunchy. Buy it from health food shops or as matzo meal from Jewish shops or delicatessens. (Not to be confused with cornflour which is used as a thickening agent.)

Cornmeal is the basis of many American southern breads, such as spoonbread, so called because it is so soft you can eat it with a spoon. The Balkan bread, *mamaliga*, is made with yellow cornmeal.

BUCKWHEAT FLOUR (GROUND BUCKWHEAT OR KASHA) This flour is used in Eastern Europe to make yeast-risen *blinis*, small, dark grey pancakes, the perfect accompaniment to caviar, smoked salmon and soured cream. An earthy and warm-flavoured flour flecked with charcoal-coloured specks. It also makes good pancakes and scones.

MILLET Add a handful of millet grains to the dough to give a pleasant crunchiness of texture. Good sprinkled on breakfast cereals too. In Roman times, wheat flour was combined with millet meal to make bread. In Britain we feed it to birds, but for people who live nearer the equator it is a staple grain and as important as wheat.

QUINOA High in protein, this grain is similar to millet. It is grown in the high Andes, and prized by the Indians. It tastes better than millet, and is often combined with potatoes.

SORGHUM This millet-like grain is not generally available in Britain though it's been a staple in parts of Africa for several thousand years.

SOYA FLOUR This flour is high in protein and used in baking to improve bread texture. A small proportion makes for a softer dough which structures well and takes up more water and air.

SEEDS

Spicy, oily, nutty seeds from flowers and grasses have been added to breads from earliest times to add interest, flavour and texture to breads. The most enduring are:

Poppy seed Purple or white poppy seeds, crunchy and smoky, sprinkled on top of a glaze give a professional finish. Characteristic of Jewish and Middle European breads.

Sesame seed An oily, white seed which toasts in the heat of the oven and gives an aromatic and chewy finish to the crust. Very popular on Middle Eastern breads.

Caraway seed A searingly pungent seed which adds piquancy and bite to Polish European breads, particularly sourdough breads. Also said to kill unwanted bacteria.

Cumin seed Cumin seed adds a haunting and mysterious scent and flavour to bread, and echoes the Middle East and India.

Sunflower seed A rich, ripe, crunchy and oily seed which can be added sparingly to a dough, especially a fruit bread. Can be sprinkled on top of the bread for a crude, rough finish.

Celery seed Sprinkle on savoury breads to give a spicy, slightly hot and bitter flavour.

Cracked wheat and kibbled wheat Sprinkle the loaf with the rough-crushed grain to get a hard, nutty, crisp shell to the loaf.

Aniseed Highly aromatic and pungent seeds to sprinkle on the top of breads, an echo of *ouzo* and Mediterranean holidays.

ENGLAND

Oatmeal Pancakes

In the Midlands these oatmeal breakfast pancakes were everyday eating at the beginning of the nineteenth century. Because oatmeal is glutinous when cooked, the finished pancakes are pliable, like wet wash-leathers. They can be stored, wrapped in a damp cloth. In Yorkshire it is usual to toast them before serving, piping hot.

MAKES ABOUT 8

4 oz fine oatmeal
4 oz medium oatmeal
½ packet activated yeast
½ pint warm water
sunflower oil for frying pancakes

- Mix the yeast with the fine oatmeal and the warm water.
- Leave to rise for 30 minutes in a warm place. Stir in 2 oz of the medium oatmeal.
- Heat a heavy frying-pan or non-stick pan until moderately hot.
- Wipe with a little sunflower oil on a piece of kitchen paper. Sprinkle on a teaspoon of the remaining oatmeal and pour in a ladleful of batter.
- Spread this out quickly with a spatula, as thinly as possible, until it is approximately 6 inches in diameter.
- When the top is dry, sprinkle with a little more of the oatmeal and turn it over to cook on the other side.
- When this too is dry, put the oat cake on a rack to cool, and repeat the process until the batter is finished. If the batter gets too thick at the bottom, add a little more water.

YEMEN

Unleavened Bread

Astonishing though it may seem, there are bedouins in Yemen and other parts of the Arab world making bread as it was made 1,000 years before Christ. They pound whole grain in a mortar, then roll it in hollowed stone hand-mills with smaller stones. Then they make flat cakes with water, cooking them on baking stones in the ashes of a fire. Sometimes they have a raising agent, where natural yeasts have started fermentation in dough which has been left for a few days. This recipe is an approximation for the kitchen. Maize flour is available in Cypriot shops and wholefood stores. Eat with soups and stews.

MAKES ABOUT 8

½ lb plain white flour (or fine maize flour)
½ lb wholemeal flour
10 fluid oz lukewarm water
pinch salt
a little olive oil, added to the dough (optional)

- Mix all the ingredients together in a bowl, then turn out and knead the dough energetically for about 10 minutes, till it feels springy and elastic.
- Cover with a damp cloth, and rest the dough for an hour.
- On a floured board, roll out little egg-sized lumps of dough into circles till very thin.
- Cook the breads under a very fierce grill, several at a time, till they puff up, about 3 minutes.
- Turn, and grill the other side, till speckled with brown dots.
- Using the same recipe, you can also fry the dough like pancakes, in a heavy iron pan or non-stick pan, one at a time.

RUSSIA

Blinis

Blinis are small yeasted pancakes made with buckwheat flour, sooty-black in colour with an earthy flavour and grainy texture. They are the perfect counterpoint to the oiliness of smoked salmon, caviar, or red salmon roe. They are equally delicious with sour cream and chopped gherkins.

SERVES 4 TO 6

8 oz buckwheat flour (or half-and-half buckwheat and plain white flour)
½ packet activated yeast
3 eggs separated
about ¾ pint milk, slightly warmed
pinch salt

- Mix the yeast with half the flour and half the milk, add the 3 yolks, beaten, and leave for half an hour to start to ferment.
- Beat in the remaining milk and flour, and leave half an hour more.
- Before cooking, whisk the whites to a froth, and fold them into the batter mixture.
- Grease a pan (non-stick is best) and fry the blinis, ladling in a dollop of mixture to produce a pancake about 4 inches wide. It will rise to ½ inch in height.
- Serve very hot.

MEXICO

Tortillas

Maize flour is the staple of Mexico, and tortillas were the bread of the country before the Spaniards introduced wheat in the sixteenth century. These flat, chewy breads, more like pancakes, are eaten at every meal. Even if the flour, *masa harina*, were readily available, which it isn't, they require a certain practice and skill to get right, and the modern Mexican woman buys them ready-made. In the north of Mexico, tortillas are made with wheat flour, and they are effective, if lacking the slight sweetness of maize.

MAKES 10 TO 12

7 oz unbleached white flour
1 teaspoon baking powder
1 teaspoon salt
1 oz butter
about ¼ pint cold water

- Sift the flour, baking powder and salt into a mixing bowl. Rub in the butter. Make a well in the centre and pour in enough water to make a stiff dough.
- Divide the dough into balls the size of small eggs.
- Roll them out on a lightly floured board, making them as thin as possible.
- Cook for about 2 minutes on each side in a heavy frying pan or non-stick pan over a medium heat.

MALAYSIA

Spring Rolls

Pastry skins bind an appetising mixture of spicy morsels of meat, seafood and fresh, crunchy vegetables. The predominant style of cooking in Malaysia is Chinese, from where spring rolls derive, and every home cook varies the ingredients to taste. Bean sprouts, though not essential, provide the crunch.

MAKES 12

12 spring roll pastry 'skins' (from a Chinese store)
½ lb beef or pork mince
1 onion, finely chopped
2 tablespoons vegetable oil
2 carrots, very finely sliced
2 oz bean sprouts
6 spring onions
soy sauce
salt and pepper
vegetable oil for deep frying

- Fry the minced meat in oil with the onions, then add the carrots.
- Take off the heat, leave to cool and mix in the bean sprouts. Season with salt, pepper and soy sauce.
- Place the mixture on the pastry skins, and roll them up neatly, tucking in the ends. (At this stage they can be frozen and stored if necessary.)
- Deep fry a few at a time in very hot oil, and drain on absorbent paper.
- Keep warm.

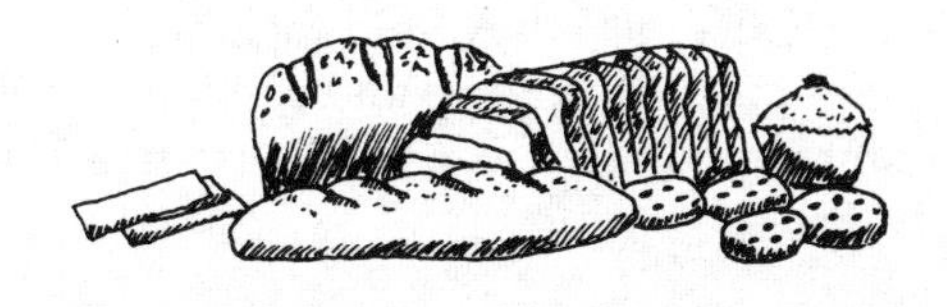

CHILE

Empanadas

Like samosas in India, the *empanada*, pastry pockets stuffed with spicy mixtures of meat, hard-boiled eggs and vegetables, is universal in South America. It is an economical dish which makes the meat go a long way, and, at the same time, is appetising, filling and nutritious.

SERVES 4

For the filling
1 tablespoon olive oil
6 oz minced (ground) beef
1 small onion, chopped
1 clove garlic, peeled and chopped
1 dried red chilli pepper, finely crumbled
pinch ground cumin
salt and pepper
2 hard-boiled eggs, cut into thin wedges
12 black olives, stoned

For the pastry
8 oz white flour
pinch salt
2 tablespoons softened lard
4 fl oz milk
vegetable oil for deep frying

- **To make the filling**, heat the oil in a frying pan and brown the meat.
- Add all the remaining ingredients except for the hard-boiled eggs and the black olives and cook over a medium heat, stirring, for 5 minutes. Cool.
- **To make the pastry**, sift the flour and salt into a large bowl. Gradually add the lard and the milk. Stir well.
- Knead the ingredients until they hold together.
- Break the dough into 2 or 3 pieces and roll them out as thinly as possible without breaking them. Cut into rounds 3–4 inches across.

- Spoon a tablespoon of meat mixture, a piece of hard-boiled egg and an olive in the centre of each circle of dough. Fold the pastry over to make a turnover, moistening the edges with a little water. Curve the turnover slightly to make a crescent shape and press the outside edges together with the prongs of a fork.
- Pour vegetable oil into a deep, heavy frying pan until it is 2 inches deep. Heat until very hot but not smoking.
- Fry the empanadas 3 or 4 at a time, until golden brown.
- Remove with a slotted spoon and drain on kitchen paper.
- Serve hot.

VENEZUELA

Arepas

These flattish rolls like small pitta breads are made from maize flour. When baked (or cooked on a griddle) they crisp up on the outside, but remain slightly doughy inside. Add 4 oz grated Gruyère cheese to the dough to make a savoury *arepa*.

MAKES 8 TO 10

8 oz masa harina (treated maize flour)
1 teaspoon salt
about 10 fl oz warm water

- Mix the flour with the salt in a bowl. Stir in the water to make a stiffish dough, adding a little more if necessary.
- Let the dough stand for 5 minutes, then form into slightly flattened balls about 3 inches across and ½ inch thick.
- Either cook on a heavy, lightly greased griddle over a moderate heat for 5 minutes each side, or bake in a hot oven, 350°F, 180°C, gas mark 4, for 20–30 minutes, turning 2 or 3 times during the cooking. They are done when they sound hollow when tapped.

INDIA

Samosas

Nourishing and tasty street food which is a good deal better for you than burgers and chips. Samosas are the most traditional snacks of India and Pakistan, eaten all day.

MAKES ABOUT 12

½ lb plain flour
pinch salt
3 or 4 tablespoons vegetable oil (ghee or clarified butter)

For the filling
½ lb potato, diced, rinsed, dried in a cloth
2 carrots, diced
4 oz peas and 4 oz French beans, cut up small
4–6 cauliflower florets
2 cloves garlic, chopped
vegetable oil (or ghee or clarified butter) for frying
1 inch fresh ginger, peeled, chopped fine
1 teaspoon turmeric
2 teaspoons garam masala
fresh coriander
vegetable oil for deep frying

- Sift the flour into a bowl with the salt. With your fingertips, rub in the ghee or oil till it looks like fine bread crumbs. Add a little water slowly, to make up a stiff dough. Press into a ball, cover or put in plastic bag, and let the pastry rest for 2 hours.
- Heat the vegetable oil (ghee or clarified butter) in a frying pan, and gently cook the vegetables for the filling for about half an hour, stirring in the spices. Leave to cool.
- On a floured board, roll out the pastry thinly, cutting into 6 large circles. Cut each one in half. Wet the straight edge of the pastry and fold over to make a cone shape, pressing the edges together with a fork to make a firm seal. Put in a blob of the filling, wet the edges and seal.
- Heat the cooking oil in a deep pan and when very hot, deep fry the samosas in batches until golden.

THAILAND

Thai Samosas

The samosa is also eaten in many other parts of the Orient. This elegant version comes from Thailand and is marvellous food for parties, picnics and buffets. Keep the filo pastry covered with a damp cloth while working, as it dries out quickly.

MAKES 24

For the samosas
3 large sheets filo pastry
1 tablespoon cornflour, mixed with hot water to make a thick paste
oil for deep frying

The filling
1 teaspoon garlic, roughly chopped
1 teaspoon coriander root (if available), roughly chopped
1 teaspoon whole black peppercorns
2 tablespoons oil
3 oz sweet potato, finely diced (or waxy potatoes)
1 large onion, finely diced
2 carrots, finely diced
3 oz boiled sweetcorn (off the cob) (or frozen, or canned)
1 teaspoon curry powder (home-made is best)
1 tablespoon light soy sauce
1 teaspoon sugar

- Pound together the garlic, coriander root and peppercorns in a mortar to form a paste.
- Heat the oil, briefly fry the potato then add the other ingredients in turn, stirring constantly. Set aside.
- Cut the filo pastry sheets into 8 short strips. Put a dab of mixture on the edge nearest you. Fold up an edge diagonally to form a triangle, then the other edges, dabbing cornflour paste on the final corner. Fold over the seal.
- Heat the oil and deep-fry the samosas until they are golden.

CHINA

Steamed Dumplings
Dim Sum

Bread isn't eaten in China, and indeed there is little history of using ovens at all, but this hasn't stopped them making puffy, sticky buns and rolls by steaming them. There is no better example of this art form than the lunchtime appetisers, *dim sum*, steamed in layers of bamboo wicker baskets, and served in restaurants in dozens of different forms, from a trolley. Fillings are legion – from jellied duck's feet to seasoned prawns. This is a typical filling with pork. This is a traditional recipe. The Chinese cookery writer, Ken Hom, says there is no reason why you shouldn't use wonton wrappers (they can be bought from Chinese stores) and they give you a slightly lighter result and with considerably less effort.

MAKES 16

For the filling
4 oz lean pork, finely chopped
1 tablespoon peanut oil
1 tablespoon onion, finely chopped
2 oz mushrooms, finely chopped
pinch salt
½ teaspoon soya sauce
1 teaspoon cornflour
1 teaspoon oyster sauce
2 tablespoons cold water

For the dumplings
8 oz white flour
2 teaspoons baking powder
1 teaspoon sugar
1 tablespoon sesame (or peanut) oil
4 fl oz warm water

- First prepare the filling by frying the pork quickly for about 1 minute in the heated peanut oil. This seals in the juices.
- Add the onion and mushrooms, stir well and cook for 1 minute. Season with salt and soya sauce.
- Mix the cornflour with the oyster sauce and cold water. Blend into the ingredients in the frying-pan and cook for 1 more minute. Remove from the heat.
- Mix the flour with the baking powder, add the sugar, oil and enough warm water to make a stiff dough. Knead on a floured board until springy.
- Divide the dough into 16 pieces, shape each into a ball, then roll out into 2½–3 inch circles.
- Put a teaspoon of filling on each circle. Moisten the edges and pinch together. Arrange the parcels on a piece of moist cloth in a steamer or place each in the steamer on a piece of greaseproof paper cut to size.
- Steam over a high heat for 12–15 minutes.
- Serve with soya sauce.

FRANCE

Pissaladière

This juicy, sweet, onion tart is a speciality of the south of France, the flavour sharpened with salty anchovies and earthy black olives. It is easy to eat, but cooking the onions very, very gently requires some patience. This is a pastry base, but you can use the same filling on a pizza base.

SERVES 4

For the pastry
6 oz flour
3 oz butter (or half-and-half lard)
pinch salt

For the filling
2 lb large mild onions (Spanish)
4 fl oz olive oil
1 lb tomatoes
1 can anchovy fillets in oil
1 dozen black olives

- Cut the fat into small pieces, and in a bowl rub into the flour with your fingertips, adding the salt. Add 1–2 tablespoons cold water, as little as possible to make a firm mass. Wrap in cling film and chill in the fridge for 1 hour at least.
- Gently fry the onions in a heavy pan or non-stick frying pan for 30 minutes or more till delicate, pale and soft. Season with salt and pepper.
- Roll out the pastry to the size of a convenient square or round baking tin, 9–10 inches across, fill with the onions and chopped tomatoes. Decorate in a criss-cross lattice with the drained anchovy fillets and stoned, black olives.
- Drizzle with more olive oil and bake in a very hot, preheated oven, 425°F, 220°C, gas mark 7, for 10 minutes, then lower the heat to 350°F, 180°C, gas mark 4, and cook for another 20 minutes, or until done.

ITALY

Home-Made Pasta

You can make pasta without a pasta machine but it's much easier and much more fun with one. What you can't do is make pasta without decent Italian pasta flour and you have to get this from an Italian store. Once you've made good fresh pasta (and you shouldn't necessarily expect it to be brilliant first time – practice makes perfect) you'll never want the bought sort.

SERVES 2

6 oz plain flour (double zero (00) in Italian stores)
2 large eggs
pinch salt
1 tablespoon olive oil, if using a blender

- Sieve the flour and salt on to a board and make a well in the middle. Beat in the eggs with a fork, drawing the flour to the middle with your other hand. Press into a ball and knead with the heels of your hand, pushing away from you, making repeated quarter turns, folding and kneading for 10 minutes.
- Alternatively, whiz all the ingredients including the oil for 15 seconds in a blender, then roll into a ball, using a few drops of water if necessary. Knead as above for 3 or 4 minutes, adding more flour if the dough is sticky. Cover with cling film for at least 30 minutes.
- Divide into 4, and on a well-floured board, with a floured rolling pin, roll out thinly, lifting and turning to help stretch.
- Cover with a cloth and leave for 5 minutes.
- Roll up the pieces and cut into fine ribbons (*fettuccine* or *tagliatelle*).
- Use at once or dry over a kitchen chair or clothes line, to cook later.
- Cook in fast-boiling, salted water for 3 or 4 minutes.

MONGOLIA

Handmade Pasta

This unsophisticated pasta, made from a soft flour and water dough and put to dry out in the sun, has been known to many races across Asia. It is made in Iran, in the Caucasus, in the Balkans (where it's called *trahana*). The Austrians and Germans have a richer version (*spatzle*). This is a simple recipe, and would be cooked in a soup, or added to a soup.

SERVES 4

8 oz white flour
1 egg, lightly beaten
pinch salt
water

- On a marble surface (or in a bowl) make a pyramid of the flour with the salt added, and make a well in the centre. Pour the egg into the middle, and stir it into the flour in a circling motion. Add a tablespoon of water if necessary to make a stiff, workable paste. Knead for 10 minutes.
- Leave uncovered for 15 minutes to dry a little, then using a grater, shred on to a floured board, using a fork to separate the strands, so they don't stick together.
- Spread on baking sheets and dry out in a warm oven. When firm, shake in a colander to get rid of small grains. Store in airtight jars, or cook at once in plenty of boiling salted water, for 10 minutes, tasting for doneness. They should be soft on the outside, *al dente* in the middle.
- Serve with butter or oil or with any accompaniment suitable for pasta; olives, anchovies, tomato sauce, and crumbled white cheese. Or add to soups and stews, adding in the last 10 minutes of cooking.

ITALY

Pasta with Clam Sauce
Linguine Vongole

A perfect sauce for pasta, juicy, succulent and savoury. Tinned clams can be bought in speciality shops.

SERVES 4

12 oz linguine (or spaghetti or tagliatelle)
4 pints clams, or mussels, or 1 can shelled clams (vongole)
2 lb tomatoes, skinned, deseeded, chopped (or 2 cans tomatoes, strained, deseeded)
1 onion, finely chopped
1 glass dry white wine
2 cloves garlic, finely chopped
parsley, chopped
4 tablespoons olive oil
salt and pepper

- Scrub the clams (or mussels) discarding any with broken shells and those which don't close when tapped.
- Put them in a heavy saucepan with the wine and chopped onion, cover and shaking occasionally, cook over a high heat until they open (5 minutes or so).
- Remove them with a slotted spoon and, when cool, remove them from their shells, keeping a few for the garnish.
- Boil the juices in the pan until reduced by half, and strain.
- In a large pan, fry the garlic in the olive oil for 30 seconds. Add the tomatoes and simmer for 15 minutes, stirring.
- Now add the clams and their juice, and the chopped parsley.
- Heat through, seasoning to taste.
- In fast-boiling, salted water, cook the pasta until *al dente*.
- Strain into a warmed bowl and pour on the sauce, garnishing with the remaining clams and a little parsley.

ITALY

Little Ears of Pasta
Orecchiette

This pasta is slightly tougher and more chewy than most, and you need to buy it from an Italian store to get the real thing. Asking for it is difficult, as Italian assistants will not understand you if you don't get it exactly right. Phonetically its 'oh-ray-kee-etty'. Having bought it, make this marvellous dish of contrasting textures, colours and flavours. While buying *orecchiette*, also get some *pancetta* ('pan-chetta') which is the rich-tasting, fatty bacon which has been cured, unlike British bacon, without the benefit of injected water.

SERVES 4

1 lb broccoli, cut into very small florets
12 oz orecchiette, or pasta shells
6 tablespoons olive oil
1 thick slice pancetta or streaky bacon, finely diced
2 cloves garlic, peeled and finely sliced
salt and pepper
grated Pecorino or Parmesan cheese
salt

- Cook the pasta rapidly in plenty of salted boiling water for 12–15 minutes, till soft but chewy inside (*al dente*).
- After 10 minutes add the broccoli, bringing it back to the boil quickly.
- Meanwhile, gently fry the pancetta in the olive oil until transparent, then add the garlic. Keep the heat low and do not let the garlic brown. Remove the garlic (unless you don't mind the extra bite, which can be fierce).

- Drain the pasta and broccoli and in a warmed bowl, swirl the olive oil and pancetta mixture to coat it well. Sprinkle generously with grated cheese.
- Serve extra olive oil at the table.

ITALY

Spaghetti with Anchovies
Spaghetti alla Puttanesca

A very pungent, strong-flavoured dressing to spaghetti. It is hot and quick, and is said to come from the poor quarter of Naples, renowned for its prostitutes, hence the name. *Puttana* is a prostitute.

SERVES 4

12 oz spaghetti
12 oz fresh tomatoes, peeled, deseeded, sliced
4 oz large black olives, stoned and sliced
4 salted anchovies (or 8 canned fillets) chopped
1 tablespoon capers
2 cloves garlic, finely sliced
1 tablespoon parsley, chopped
6 tablespoons olive oil
1 dried red chilli (or more to taste), crumbled
salt

- Drop the spaghetti into rapidly boiling, salted water.
- In a large frying pan, cook the anchovies, garlic and red chilli in the oil for 1 minute. Add the tomatoes, olives and capers and cook for a couple of minutes more. Taste and adjust the seasoning.
- When the spaghetti is *al dente* (after about 10 minutes) drain and stir it into the pan with the sauce, adding the parsley.
- Cook for 1 minute, stirring to mix thoroughly.
- Serve at once.

CHINA

Chow Mein

Many Chinese eat noodles several times a day – in soup, mixed with braised meat in sauces, or as a garnish to a stir-fry of meat, chicken, seafood or vegetables. Freshly made noodles are tastiest, but dried wheat or egg noodles are fine.

Fresh noodles cook in 2 or 3 minutes, dried noodles in 5 or 6 – less time than it takes to microwave many 'quick', ready-made dishes. Allow 4 oz per person (which gives a cooked weight of ½ lb each). Plunge the noodles into plenty of boiling water, being careful not to let it froth over. Boil them for 5 minutes but don't overcook. Drain and rinse.

SERVES 4

1 lb egg noodles
6 oz lean pork
6 oz chicken breast
½ lb each of onions, carrots, broccoli, celery
5 spring onions, chopped
1 teaspoon chilli sauce
groundnut oil
1 pint chicken stock (or cube)

For the marinade
2 tablespoons soy sauce
2 tablespoons cornflour
1 inch grated ginger
2 cloves chopped garlic

- To make the meat easier to cut, wrap it in clingfilm and chill in the freezer for 30 minutes.
- Slice into medallions ⅛ inch thick and put in a bowl with the marinade for at least 30 minutes.
- Prepare the vegetables, slicing diagonally, and blanch the carrots then plunge into cold water.
- Drain. Boil the noodles for 5 minutes, drain, rinse and reserve.
- Heat the wok. Add the groundnut oil and cook the marinated meat for 2 or 3 minutes. Reserve.

- Rinse the pan and re-heat. Add a little more oil and, when it is smoking, stir-fry all the vegetables for 2 or 3 minutes.
- Add the stock, simmer for 2 minutes, stir in the meat and heat.
- Set aside half the mixture on a warm serving plate.
- Combine the noodles with the ingredients left in the pan, adding the spring onions, soy sauce and chilli sauce.
- When piping hot, add the reserved ingredients.

ITALY

Gnocchi

These little shapes of cooked semolina, with ham, cheese and a tomato sauce, provide a comforting, homely meal.

SERVES 4

4 oz semolina
¼ pint milk
¾ pint water
1 small onion (stuck with 2 cloves)
bay leaf
grated nutmeg
2 oz ham, finely chopped
2 oz Parmesan cheese, grated
home-made tomato sauce (see pizza recipe on page 132)
sprig parsley, finely chopped
olive oil

- Heat the milk and water with the flavourings of onion, bay leaf and pinch of grated nutmeg, and simmer for 5 minutes.
- Discard the flavourings, add the semolina, stirring to prevent it forming lumps, and cook gently for 5 minutes.
- Off the heat stir in the ham, the parsley and half the cheese.
- Spread the mixture on to an oiled baking sheet or plate with a spatula (dipped in boiling water) to a thickness of ½ inch.
- When cool, cut the mixture into squares, and arrange in overlapping layers in an oiled, heat-proof dish.
- Sprinkle with the remainder of the cheese, drizzle with olive oil, and brown under a grill for 10 minutes. Serve with tomato sauce.

ROMANIA

Mamaliga

This cornmeal 'cake' is the national dish of Romania, eaten by country people as their staple food. It is known as 'bread of gold', descriptive of its sunny yellow colour. You can either eat it from the cooking pan, spooned like porridge on to your plate as a starchy accompaniment to savoury dishes, soups and stews, or pour it into an oiled mould to set as a slab, or on to an oiled sheet of foil and patted flat to a thickness of ½ or ¾ inch and left to cool. You can then use slices for grilling or frying, or cut into cubes and bake with a cheese or tomato sauce, like Italian gnocchi.

SERVES 4 TO 6

8 oz cornmeal
1¾ pints water
2 teaspoons salt

- Boil the water and salt in a large saucepan.
- Add the cornmeal a handful at a time, letting a golden rain trickle slowly through your fingers. Stir all the time as you add it, using a long-handled wooden spoon, because the boiling mixture may spit. Continue adding the cornmeal slowly or it will go into lumps.
- When the mixture is smooth and thick, cover the pan, lower the heat and continue cooking gently for 30 minutes.
- Serve it straight from the pan as a starchy alternative to potatoes or rice, or turn it out on to a wooden board and spread it flat with a palette knife dipped in boiling water, leave to cool and use, as described above.

ROMANIA

Fried Mamaliga

What to do with cold polenta, if you make too much to eat hot with your main meal. Pour the surplus into a small, greased loaf-tin. When cold, turn it out, and cut into slices to grill with cheese, bake with a tomato or cheese sauce, or fry, dipped in egg.

SERVES 4

4 slices mamaliga (see previous recipe on page 130)
1 egg, beaten
2 oz cheese, grated
oil (or butter) for frying
4 oz carton plain yoghurt, or sour cream

- Coat slices of mamaliga in beaten egg.
- Dip them into the cheese, covering both sides generously.
- Fry in oil, or butter, till brown on both sides.
- Serve hot with yoghurt or sour cream.

To bake with cheese sauce, to serve 4

- Make a roux, melting 1 oz butter and stirring in 1 oz flour.
- Pour in ½ pint warmed milk, slowly and stirring to avoid lumps.
- Cook for 5 minutes then add 4 oz grated cheese and 1 teaspoon mustard.
- Cut mamaliga into 1 inch cubes, cover with sauce and bake in a hot oven for 15–20 minutes, till bubbling.
- Sprinkle with breadcrumbs and finish under the grill for a crisp finish.

ITALY

Pizza

Pizza, as cooked in Naples, which is where it originates, is deliciously simple, a million miles from the pizza parlour specials with endless toppings. They serve it with red tomato sauce, a blob of melting white mozzarella cheese, and a green leaf of basil, making up the colours of the Italian flag. If you can't get fresh basil, use fresh or dried oregano. Don't deny yourself the savoury bite of some anchovies and olives. In a children's version add flaked tuna or sliced pepperoni.

SERVES 4

For the dough
1 lb plain white flour
1 packet activated yeast
½ pint warm water
2 tablespoons olive oil
1 teaspoon salt

For the filling
*½ pint thick tomato sauce**
4 oz mozzarella (or melting) cheese
1 dozen stoned, black olives
fresh basil leaves (or oregano)
(optional: anchovy fillets, 2 oz tinned tuna, shredded, slices of pepperoni)

****Tomato sauce***
2 cans tomatoes, chopped
2 cloves garlic
olive oil
salt and pepper

- Crush and chop the garlic.
- Fry in olive oil till it starts to colour. Add the tomato, salt and pepper and simmer on a low heat for up to 30 minutes, to get a thickish, soupy mixture. Leave it to cool.

- In a bowl mix the flour, yeast, salt, oil and water to an elastic dough. Knead until springy and elastic, about 10 minutes. Dust with flour and put it in a plastic bag, leaving room for the dough to expand.
- Put it in a warm place to rise, and leave till doubled in size, between 1 and 2 hours.
- Cut the dough into 4, make into balls, then roll out into circles about 8–10 inches across. Too thin, and the crust is like a biscuit; too thick and it's all dough. (You can roll it out into large squares on a baking sheet with raised edges, if that is more convenient.)
- Spoon equal amounts of the cool tomato sauce on to each pizza base, adding cut circles of mozzarella which will melt into pools.
- Add the anchovies, olives and other fillings to taste, sprinkle with torn leaves of basil, or oregano, drizzle with a little extra olive oil and bake in a preheated hot oven, 450°F, 230°C, gas mark 8, for 15 minutes, till sizzling and eat at once.

YUGOSLAVIA

Quick Pizza

Pogaça

This quick recipe from the north of the former Yugoslavia, close to the Italian border, doesn't respect Italian traditions. On a belt and braces principle, it employs two raising agents, yeast and self-raising flour. Children love it.

SERVES 4

1 lb self-raising flour
½ pint milk
1 packet quick yeast
1 teaspoon salt
½ bottle tomato ketchup (or home-made tomato sauce)
4 oz cheese, sliced
some slices of red or green pepper (or any fillings of your choice – ham, tuna, salami, peas)
dried oregano
olive oil

- Warm the milk slightly and mix it with the flour, yeast and salt in a bowl. On a floured board, make it into a ball of dough, and knead well. Place it in covered bowl and leave in a warm place for 30 minutes to rise.
- Heat the oven to very hot (450°F, 230°C, gas mark 8).
- Oil a flat baking tray, and press out the dough on to it with your hands, flattening it as you go, using your thumbs to make a raised ridge around the edges.
- Spread the tomato sauce across the surface, then the slices of cheese and the sliced peppers, and sprinkle with oregano (or dried basil or marjoram), and dribble with olive oil.
- Bake the pizza in a hot oven for 20 minutes till sizzling.

LEBANON

Pitta Bread

Flat pitta breads make the most perfect sandwiches, split to open up the pocket and stuffed full of crispy salad. In the Middle East it is the everyday form of bread, often eaten dipped in a spice mixture called *zahter*, which is often sold in the street wrapped in cones of paper. It is not difficult to make pitta bread at home.

MAKES 8 PITTA BREADS

1 lb plain white flour
1 packet activated yeast
½ teaspoon salt
½ pint warm water
1 tablespoon olive oil

- Mix the flour, yeast, salt, oil and water with a wooden spoon in a bowl. Knead for 10 minutes. Smooth a little more oil over the outside of the dough and leave it to rise in a warm place for 2 hours, well covered.
- Knock the dough down, cut it into 8 pieces and work each piece into a ball.
- Cover again and leave to prove for half an hour.
- Preheat the oven to 230°C, 450°F, gas mark 8.
- Knead each ball of dough and roll on a floured board into 8 ovals. Put them on greased and floured baking sheets and let them prove for a further 30 minutes, covered with a cloth.
- Brush with cold water and bake on greased sheets for 10 minutes, removing while still pale. Wrap in a cloth to keep them soft.
- Eat when cool or reheat later.

TRINIDAD

Roti

The delicious Indian bread eaten with curries. This recipe is from the Caribbean. When slavery was abolished in the West Indies, plantation owners hired labour from India.

MAKES ABOUT 4 LARGE ROTI

½ lb wholemeal flour	*1 teaspoon salt*
1 packet activated yeast (½ oz fresh yeast)	*1½ oz butter*
	2 oz clarified butter, melted

- Mix the flour, yeast and salt in a bowl. Rub in the butter with your fingertips until the mixture resembles breadcrumbs. Make a well in the centre and pour in the yeast liquid. Mix thoroughly with a wooden spoon, then knead to make a fairly stiff dough.
- Add more water, 1 tablespoon at a time, until the dough becomes softer and more elastic but is not sticky. Knead well. Cover the dough and leave for 30 minutes.
- Knead again for 3 to 4 minutes, then divide into 4 balls. Roll out on a floured board into 12 or 8 inch rounds as desired.
- Brush lightly all over with clarified butter and sprinkle with flour. Fold them in half twice so that they form a 4-layered quarter-circle. Cover and leave for 30 minutes.
- Roughly shape the roti into circles with the hands and roll out on a floured board into 12 or 8 inch rounds. Heat a cast-iron frying pan or non-stick pan to hot.
- Place one of the roti in the pan and cook for about 1 minute. Turn and spread it with a thin layer of melted clarified butter.
- Cook it for another 2 minutes and spread again with the butter.
- Cook for a minute longer and turn.
- Cook for a minute on this side, and remove from the pan to a board. Hit it all over with a wooden mallet until it is flaky.
- Wrap the roti in a towel until the other roti are cooked.

RUSSIA AND USA

Bagels

Half-way between a bread and a biscuit, they are unique in being boiled first, which expands the dough, then baked, to crisp them up. They originate in Eastern Europe, where they were strung together through their holes, like quoits, and sold at fairs. They entered the Jewish tradition, and there is no treat quite like bagels with smoked salmon and sour cream.

MAKES 12

12 oz white flour
1 packet activated yeast
5 fl oz lukewarm water
1½ teaspoons salt
2 tablespoons honey (or sugar)
4 tablespoons oil
1 egg
7 pints boiling water
1 tablespoon cold water
poppy seeds or caraway seeds
1 egg yolk diluted with 2 teaspoons cold water, to glaze

- Sift the flour, salt and yeast into a bowl. Beat the egg and oil into the warm water and stir into the flour. Make into a firm, smooth dough. Knead for 3–4 minutes. Cover with a cloth and leave in a warm place to rise for 1 hour.
- Turn out on to a floured board, and knead well until the dough acquires elasticity.
- Divide the dough into 12 equal pieces and shape each into a roll about 5 inches long and ¾ inch thick. Make these into rings, pinching the ends together and smoothing them out as evenly as possible. Leave covered on a floured board for 10–15 minutes.
- Add the honey (or sugar) to the boiling water in a very large, wide saucepan and bring to a rolling boil.

- Drop the bagels in one by one. When they are all in the saucepan (or as many as will fit in) and the water has been brought back to the boil, reduce the heat and allow the bagels to simmer gently for 10–15 minutes, until they float.
- Remove the bagels with a slotted spoon and drain well on kitchen paper. Place them on a greased baking sheet and brush each with a diluted egg yolk to glaze. Sprinkle with the seeds.
- Bake for 25–30 minutes in a preheated oven, 400°F, 200°C, gas mark 6, until smooth, crisp and golden brown.

ENGLAND

Crumpets

Crumpets were once the glory of the English high tea. They are surprisingly easy to make. The dough is quite sloppy and slack and the bubbly texture is achieved by using both yeast and baking powder. You only cook one side, leaving the top uncooked to be toasted later.

MAKES ABOUT 12 CRUMPETS

1 lb strong plain flour
½ lb packet activated yeast
1 pint of warm water
1 teaspoon baking powder
1 teaspoon sugar
1 teaspoon salt

- Put the flour in a mixing bowl with the yeast, salt and baking powder, and beat in warm water gradually, until creamier than a dough but not as runny as a batter. Leave to stand for 1½–2 hours in a warm place.
- Cook the crumpets on a greased hotplate (set to low) or in a heavy greased pan or non-stick pan. The batter should be poured into crumpet rings, which are like circular pastry cutters, or you can make 1 large crumpet the size of a dinner plate, and cut it into squares after cooking, as they do in the north of England. The crumpets are ready after 8–10 minutes. Don't turn.

ENGLAND

Muffins

Muffins died out for a while, but they are now reappearing in some bakeries. They were traditionally sold by street-sellers from trays they carried on their heads, leaving one hand free to ring a bell to announce their wares. They make an unusual alternative to soft rolls or scones for tea.

MAKES 16 MUFFINS

1 lb strong plain flour
10 oz warm milk
1 packet activated yeast
1 egg
1 teaspoon sugar
1 oz melted butter
1 teaspoon salt

- Dissolve the yeast in the warm milk and stir in the sugar to help activate the yeast. In 10 minutes it should start to froth and be ready to use.
- Mix the flour and the yeast and milk mixture. Stir in the beaten egg and the butter, and add the salt.
- Knead this dough on a floured surface for about 10 minutes, till it is light and elastic. Make it into a rounded lump, place it on a greased baking sheet, and cover with a plastic bag. Leave it till it doubles in size (less than half an hour in a warm kitchen).
- Cut the dough into pieces and roll them into rounds 3 inches across and ¾ inch thick. Return them to the greased sheet, and leave to rise a second time, for about 20 minutes.
- Cook the muffins over a low heat on a lightly-oiled griddle, or in a buttered frying pan, for 8 minutes on each side, or bake in a low oven, 325°F, 160°C, gas mark 3, for 20 minutes. They double in size, and are ready when lightly browned.
- Serve at once, split in half and buttered, or with jam and cream like scones for tea. Muffins are also delicious the following day, toasted.

IRELAND

Soda Bread

Surely one of the glories of the Irish kitchen. Baking soda is the activating agent, and because the dough does not have to be left to rise like yeasty breads, you can start baking as soon as the oven is hot. Even quicker are scones made from the mixture, the ideal solution when friends drop in unexpectedly for tea.

Every housewife in the west of Ireland makes this like a dream and I don't know if it's lovelier eaten warm with freshly churned Irish butter, at tea with home-made jams and curds, or with oysters and salty-sweet smoked salmon. It may be practice makes perfect but I've never tasted such good soda bread outside Ireland. Certainly it is worth using only the best, fresh stoneground flour.

MAKES 1 LARGE LOAF

1½ lb wholemeal flour (or half wholemeal, half white)
1 pint buttermilk (or sour milk)
3 level teaspoons bicarbonate soda
6 level teaspoons cream of tartar
2 oz butter, diced
2 level teaspoons honey (or black treacle, or brown sugar)

- Rub the butter into the flour. Blend with the cream of tartar, bicarbonate of soda and the salt. Add the honey to the milk and mix with the flour to a soft dough. Some flours take up more liquid than others, so it is difficult to be absolutely exact.
- Pat into a flattish round loaf and place on a greased baking sheet.
- Cut through the dough with a knife into quarters.
- Bake for about 30 minutes in a preheated oven, 400°F, 200°C, gas mark 8.

ITALY

Onion Bread

The onions, fried gently to sweetness, gives this bread a melting richness. This recipe comes from Tuscany.

MAKES 2 SMALL LOAVES

1¾ lb strong white flour
1 packet activated yeast (1 oz fresh)
2 large onions
½ pint milk
2 tablespoons sunflower oil
1½ teaspoons salt
½ oz butter
1 egg

- Peel and chop the onions very finely. Heat the oil in a frying pan, add the onions and cook over a moderately low heat, stirring every now and then, until they are well browned and crisp. Drain the onions on kitchen paper.
- Warm the flour in a basin with the yeast and salt.
- Add the butter, cut into small pieces, and rub it into the flour until the mixture resembles fine breadcrumbs.
- Add the onions and mix well.
- Make a well in the centre of the flour, add the milk and stir the flour into the liquid until the mixture forms a firm dough.
- Turn on to a floured board and knead until smooth and elastic. Place in an oiled bowl, cover with a damp cloth and leave in a warm, draught-proof place to rise for 1 hour.
- Punch the dough down, place in 2 oiled 1 lb tins, cover with a damp cloth and leave to rise again for a further 45 minutes.
- Brush the loaves with beaten egg and bake for about 20 minutes in a hot oven, preheated to 450°F, 230°C, gas mark 8, until golden brown and sounding hollow when tapped on the bottom. Turn on to a wire rack to cool.
- You can also bake this dough in the form of plaits, or make it into rolls.

BELGIUM

Wholemeal Bread

The dough for this loaf only requires one rising. After kneading, put it into the tin and put in a warm place.

MAKES 1 LOAF

4 oz strong white flour
12 oz wholemeal flour
1 packet activated yeast
1 oz butter
2 teaspoons salt

- Lightly grease a 1 lb loaf tin with a little butter.
- Sift the white flour, yeast and salt into a bowl and stir in the wholemeal flour. Make a well in the centre and pour in the water.
- Cut the rest of the butter into small pieces, arrange them round the edge of the mixture and gradually draw the flour into the liquid with your fingers. Keep mixing in this way until no loose flour remains and the dough leaves the sides of the bowl cleanly.
- Turn out the dough on to a floured surface and knead for 10 minutes. Make it into a loaf shape and place in the prepared tin.
- Cover the tin with a clean, damp cloth and leave in a warm place for 20 minutes or until the dough has risen to the top of the tin.
- Preheat the oven to 400°F, 200°C, gas mark 6, and bake for 25 minutes. After 5 minutes reduce the heat to 375°F, 190°C, gas mark 5.
- If the loaf does not sound hollow when tapped after this time, further reduce the heat to 350°F, 180°C, gas mark 4, and put the loaf back for another 5–10 minutes.

ENGLAND

The Grant Loaf

This celebrated loaf was created by Doris Grant, the food reformer, in desperation to provide an alternative to the ubiquitous white sliced loaf of post-war years. The intention was to put back some of the fibre lacking in the modern diet. It's a no-knead, sloppy, wet dough, which cooks to quite a heavy cake. A couple of slices a day suffices.

MAKES 3 LOAVES

3 lb stoneground wholemeal flour
1 pack activated yeast
2 pints lukewarm water
2 scant teaspoons salt

- Put the flour and yeast into a large bowl and add the salt. In very cold weather, warm the flour slightly, just enough to take off the chill.
- Mix well – by hand is best – working from the sides of the bowl to the middle, till the dough feels elastic and leaves the sides of the bowl clean.
- Divide the dough, which should be slippery but not wet, between three 2 pint bread tins, warmed and greased.
- Cover the tins with a cloth and put in a warm place for about 20 minutes, or until the dough is within ½ inch from the top of the tins.
- Preheat the oven to 400°F, 200°C, gas mark 6, and bake for 35–40 minutes.

GERMANY

Pumpernickel

Moist, dark, crumbly pumpernickel is a dense, but delicious, alternative to biscuits or rolls. Use it as an open sandwich with salad, tomatoes, eggs, ham and savoury morsels. In factories it is steamed in tin bread moulds. This recipe can be made at home and gives a reasonable version. Store pumpernickel wrapped in foil to keep it moist.

MAKES 2 SMALL LOAVES

1½ lb rye flour
1½ packets activated yeast
2 oz butter
¾ pint warm milk
5 tablespoons molasses or black treacle
1 egg, beaten
1 teaspoon salt
2 tablespoons caraway seeds
2 tablespoons cream for glaze

- Melt the butter in the warm milk.
- When it cools to lukewarm, dissolve the molasses in it, adding the beaten egg and salt.
- Add the caraway seeds and ½ lb of the rye flour with the yeast. Beat until smooth. Leave this wet mixture to rise for 30 minutes.
- Mix in another ½ lb rye flour. Cover the bowl with a damp cloth and leave for 30 minutes or more to rise further.
- Now stir in the rest of the rye flour, and knead well for 10 minutes. If the dough is too sticky, add a little more flour.
- Make the dough into 2 ovals, and press them into 2 greased 1 lb baking tins until they come up to the halfway mark. Cover with a dry cloth and leave to prove for 1 hour.
- Bake for 40 minutes in an oven preheated to 400°F, 200°C, gas mark 6. After 30 minutes, brush the tops with cream.
- Remove the loaves and cool them on a wire tray. Do not eat until the bread is cold.

DENMARK

Rye Bread

The dense, chewy texture of rye bread cut thinly is an ideal base for Scandinavian *smörrebrod*, which means no more than buttered bread, or 'smeared' bread, not to be confused with *smörgåsbord*, the Swedish buffet table of dozens of cold (and hot) dishes. The Danish 'open sandwiches' are usually arranged very elegantly with crisp lettuce, squares of tasty cheese, ham, egg, or delicious prawns fresh from Arctic waters.

MAKES 2 LARGE LOAVES

2 lb rye flour
7 oz strong plain flour
2 tablespoons black treacle
½ pint milk
½ pint water
2 packets activated yeast
1 tablespoon salt

- Mix the flours together with the yeast and salt in a large mixing bowl.
- Dissolve the treacle in ½ pint hot water and mix with the cold milk.
- Stir into the flour and mix to a dough with a wooden spoon, then knead for about 5 minutes on a floured board.
- Oil two large bread tins. Divide the dough into 2, shape each into a roll, and put them in the tins, pricking them all the way through with a fork in several places. Put the tins in a lightly oiled, polythene bag, and leave to rise for about 2½ hours.
- Bake in a very hot oven preheated to 450°F, 230°C, gas mark 7, for 15 minutes, then reduce the heat to 400°F, 200°C, gas mark 6, and bake for another 45–50 minutes. (For a crusty loaf, remove the bread from the tins 15 minutes before the end.)
- Allow the loaves to cool completely on a wire tray, then wrap them in a polythene bag, and keep for a day before slicing.

WALES

Barley Bread

The Welsh (and English) working folk ate barley bread or a bread with a mixture of grains (*maslin*) while the aristocracy enjoyed ever more and more refined versions of white wheaten bread. Barley gives a greyish colour, but imparts a delicious flavour. The bread soon becomes quite dry so needs to be wrapped to keep the moisture in. In Wales dry barley bread was added to soups. If you can't get barley flour you can mill your own from whole barley grain in a wiped-clean coffee grinder, several batches at a time.

MAKES 1 LARGE LOAF (OR 2 SMALL ONES)

1 lb strong white (bread) flour
4 oz barley flour
¾ pint warm (not hot) water
3 tablespoons buttermilk (or creamy milk)
1 teaspoon of salt

- Mix the two flours with the yeast and salt in a bowl. Make a well in the centre and stir in the water with a wooden spoon. Turn the mixture out on to a floured board, and roll it into a ball with your hands. Dust the dough with flour, return to the bowl, cover with clingfilm or a plastic bag, and put it in a warm, not hot, place. Leave 1½–2 hours to expand to twice its original volume.
- Punch down the dough and knead it briefly. Put it in a greased bread tin (capacity 3½ pints) to rise till doubled in size.
- Preheat the oven to hot, 425°F, 220°C, gas mark 7, and bake the bread for 15 minutes, then reduce the heat to 400°F, 200°C, gas mark 6, for another 15 minutes.

- Shake the loaf from its tin and return it on its side to the oven, turned down to 350°F, 180°C, gas mark 4, for a further 15–20 minutes. It is baked when the loaf gives out a hollow sound when you tap the sides and the bottom.
- Leave to cool on a rack.

USA

Spoon Bread

This sweetcorn bread belongs to the old colonial tradition, when the first settlers were adapting to the maize flour used by the Indians. It's more like a pudding than a loaf, and should be eaten while still hot and moist, from the oven.

SERVES 4

6 oz fine cornmeal
1 oz butter
1 pint buttermilk (or sour milk)
3 medium eggs, beaten
1 teaspoon baking powder
¼ teaspoon bicarbonate of soda
½ teaspoon salt

- Sift the cornmeal, baking powder, bicarbonate of soda and salt together into a mixing bowl. Make a well in the centre and pour in the beaten eggs.
- Put either a 8 × 8 × 2 inch baking tin or large soufflé dish in a moderately hot oven (400°F, 200°C, gas mark 6) to warm, adding butter to melt.
- Mix the eggs into the cornmeal, then beat in the buttermilk.
- Remove the tin or dish from the oven and tip it to coat all inside surfaces with melted butter.
- Pour the excess butter into the batter and stir quickly to mix.
- Pour the batter into the tin or dish. Bake for 35 minutes and serve immediately.

ENGLAND

Malt Bread

Malted barley provides the starch which is turned to sugar to make gluey malt extract, a childhood treat fed to another generation as a rich source of vitamins. Vestigial traces of it's haunting sticky sweetness and it's certain smell of the farmyard linger on in modern malt breads. This is a dense, family bread, and made quickly as it contains no yeast.

MAKES 1 SMALL LOAF

8 oz white flour
1 heaped teaspoon baking powder
1 teaspoon salt
4 oz raisins or sultanas
2 oz chopped dates
½ pint milk
2 teaspoons honey
2 teaspoons malt extract
1 tablespoon black treacle

- Preheat the oven to 325°F, 170°C, gas mark 3.
- Sift the flour, baking powder and salt into a basin, and add the dried fruit.
- Put the milk, honey, malt extract and black treacle into a saucepan and stir over a low heat until lukewarm.
- Pour into the flour and dried fruit mixture, mix well, and beat to a soft dough (a wooden spoon is best).
- Grease and line a 1 lb bread tin, and press the dough into the tin.
- Bake for 1 hour.

WEST INDIES

Coconut Bread

A delightful and unusual tropical sweet bread flavoured with grated fresh coconut, lovely for tea.

MAKES 2 LOAVES

¾ lb white flour
½ lb cornmeal
1 packet activated yeast
½ pint milk (warm)
¼ lb finely grated coconut
2 large ripe bananas, mashed
¼ lb unsalted butter, melted and cooled
2 tablespoons honey
½ teaspoon ground allspice
1 teaspoon salt

- Mix the flour and cornmeal together. Mix half the flour mixture all the yeast, and the milk in a large bowl, cover with a cloth and leave in a warm place to rise for about 1½ hours, until double in size.
- Add the rest of the flour mixture and all the remaining ingredients and enough water to make a stiff batter. Beat thoroughly with a wooden spoon.
- Pour the mixture into 2 greased 9 × 5 × 3 inch loaf tins. Cover loosely with a cloth and leave in a warm place to rise for about 30 minutes.
- Preheat the oven to 350°F, 180°C, gas mark 4, and bake for 45 minutes to 1 hour, or until the bread begins to shrink from the sides of the tins and the top is lightly browned.
- Cool in the tins for a few minutes before turning out on to a wire rack.
- Serve it instead of biscuits or cakes as a morning or tea-time snack.

POLAND

Poppy Seed Roll

Polish classic cake served with morning coffee or at tea-time, or even as a dessert to finish a meal. You can enrich it with chopped nuts or dried fruit, or both.

SERVES 8

1 lb plain flour
10 oz poppy seeds
¾ pint milk
1 packet activated yeast
2 eggs
4 oz butter
6 tablespoons honey
2 tablespoons candied peel, chopped
1 teaspoon cinnamon
pinch salt

- Sift the flour yeast and salt into a large, warmed, mixing bowl. Make a well in the centre and pour in half the milk, warmed to the temperature of your hand. Work in the flour and knead to make a smooth dough. Cover the bowl with a lightly floured cloth and put it in a warm place for 1½–2 hours, until the dough doubles in size.
- Rinse the poppy seeds with hot water and drain them well (this is best done through muslin). Finely grind the seeds in a blender, or a mortar.
- In a saucepan, heat the milk, add the honey and bring gently to the boil. Add the ground poppy seeds and vanilla essence and cook, stirring frequently, until the mixture thickens.
- Stir in the candied peel, cinnamon and melted butter. Remove from the heat and leave to cool.
- Knock down the dough and work in the eggs, beating well.
- Turn it out and knead on a floured board. Then roll out the dough into a rectangle until it is just over ¼ inch thick. Moisten the edges and spread the filling thickly over the rectangle almost to the edges.

- Roll it up, place on a lightly greased baking tray, cover with a cloth and leave to rise in a warm place for a further 1½–2 hours.
- Brush the top of the poppy seed roll with the melted butter and bake in a preheated oven, 375°F, 190°C, gas mark 5, for 35–45 minutes.

SWITZERLAND

Milk Bread

Zop

Milk not only enriches bread, but it sweetens it and improves texture. This is a plaited Sunday bread, similar to Jewish *cholla*.

MAKES 1 LARGE LOAF

1 lb strong white flour
1 packet activated yeast
8 fl oz lukewarm milk
2 oz butter, melted
1 teaspoon salt
1 egg
1 egg yolk, for the glaze

- Melt the butter in the warm milk, with the salt. Gradually mix this liquid into the flour and yeast. Add the egg and knead well for about 5 minutes. Cover and leave to rise in a warm place for about 1½ hours.
- Knock back the dough and divide into 3 equal pieces.
- Shape each piece into a long, thin strip. Start to plait from the centre. Turn the loaf around and plait from the other end. Cover and set to rise a second time for about 30 minutes. Before baking, put in a cool place for 10 minutes.
- Brush the loaf with the egg yolk and bake for 45 minutes, in an oven preheated to 375°F, 190°C, gas mark 5.
- Eat instead of cakes at tea. It's tempting to serve it with plenty of butter.

INDIA

Spicy Gram Cake
Dhokra

Gram flour is not made from grain but from chickpeas, but it is by no means the only bean used as a flour: the delicious crispy soufflé of a pancake, *masala dosai*, of south India is made with the flour of the lentil, *urad dal*, and of course soy flour is not only used to make *tofu*, the Chinese and Japanese bean curd, but is also an effective flour improver used in the baking industry to improve texture.

This unusual cake is from the Gujarat, west India, esteemed for its sophisticated cuisine. It is steamed in a double boiler, and, strange to tell, the raising agent is a shot of health salts. Eat this hot, sweet, spicy cake with morning coffee or afternoon tea.

SERVES 8 TO 10

4 oz gram flour (chickpea flour)
8 oz carton plain yoghurt
Eno's health salts (or bicarbonate of soda)*
1 inch fresh ginger, grated
1 green chilli, deseeded, finely chopped
2 oz sugar
vegetable oil
1 tablespoon desiccated coconut
1 teaspoon mustard seeds (or sesame seeds)
1 teaspoon chopped coriander
vegetable oil for brushing mould

- Prepare the cake batter a day in advance.
- Mix the gram flour and yoghurt in a bowl to make the batter. Cover and leave overnight to fluff up.

- Stand a small saucepan inside a larger pan, half-filled with water, and heat over a low flame until simmering. Brush the inside of the smaller pan with ½ teaspoon oil and 1 teaspoon Eno's salts.
- Add a pinch or two of ginger, chilli and sugar to the batter.
- Stir 2 tablespoons batter into the small saucepan, cover and leave to cook for 10–15 minutes, until the batter rises.
- Spoon the risen batter into an oiled mould, 1–2 inches deep, and leave to cool.
- Repeat this process until the batter is used up.
- Cut into 1 inch squares to serve.
- Brush with oil and sprinkle with coconut, mustard seeds or sesame seeds, and chopped coriander.

*Eno's produces more carbon dioxide gas than normal baking powder.

ITALY

Ciabatta

Ciabatta, pronounced 'cha-batta', the flat loaf named after a slipper, has become the most fashionable bread in Britain. If all bread was as tasty, we would soon assume the national goal of eating more bread at the expense of high-calorie biscuits, cakes and snacks.

It's a tricky bread to make because it's impossible to knead the very wet dough and you need plenty of flour on your hands when you're shaping it. But, like learning to swim or riding a bike, it will give you a craftsman's sense of achievement when you've done it. The bread eats superbly well when fresh; when stale, ciabatta is lovely toasted, rubbed with garlic, if you like, and topped with a cut ripe tomato, drizzled with olive oil and sprinkled with sea-salt – the Catalan peasant breakfast of *pan amb oli*.

MAKES 4 FLAT LOAVES 10 × 4 INCHES

1 lb sourdough, made 12 hours previously (see note)
1 lb plain flour
¾ pint liquid (of which 4 fl oz is milk, the rest tepid water)
1 packet activated yeast (or ¼ oz fresh yeast or 1 teaspoon dry yeast)
½ oz (1 level tablespoon) salt
1 tablespoon extra virgin olive oil
cornmeal to spinkle on baking sheet

- If necessary, reconstitute the fresh or dry yeast in a cup, dissolving in a little warm water, waiting till it froths up.
- Mix all the ingredients (except cornmeal) together vigorously in a mixing bowl with a metal spoon (you can give it a 2-minute spin in a mixer, if you have one).
- With floured hands, turn out this gluey mixture into a oiled bowl, cover with clingfilm and leave for 1½ hours to double in volume.
- Clear a large space and prepare 4 pieces of baking paper (or greaseproof paper) cutting them into sheets about 12 × 6 inches.
- Toss a mass of white flour on to your worktop, and with floured hands turn out the runny dough, loosely shaping into a flat ball. Cut into 4 and, still sprinkling with flour, roll into blobs.
- Juggling them swiftly with floured hands, pull out each one into flat 10 inch lengths, 4 inches across, and lay on the well-floured baking paper.
- Prod the surface with your fingers to press out some of the air inside. The dough is now very flat, but it will re-inflate in the oven.
- Leave to rise, covered with a damp cloth, for 1½–2 hours.
- Half an hour before baking, pre-heat the oven to very hot, 425°F, 220°C, gas mark 7. Preferably, line one shelf with oven bricks to imitate the brick base of an Italian oven. But you can achieve a similar effect using a solid metal shelf.
- When you are ready to bake, sprinkle the baking surface with fine cornmeal to prevent sticking. Carefully invert the loaves on to the baking sheet in a row. Bake for 25–30 minutes. If you have a water spray (used for plants) spray the surface of the loaves several times in the first 5 minutes. This prevents the crust from baking hard too quickly, allowing the bubbles to balloon up, a characteristic of the bread.

Note on sourdough

- This is a five-day operation. Starting on Day One, grind 1 oz organic wheat to flour (or simply use 1 oz organic white flour) and mix in a cup with 1 oz tepid water. Cover with cling-film, and stand in the kitchen (in neither a very hot nor very cold place) for 3 days. When it begins to 'work', small bubbles will appear, and the mixture will give off a yeasty, cheesy smell.

- On Day Four, add 3 oz white flour, and 3 oz warm water, mix, and cover; it should start to work slowly – this is a natural leaven, and doesn't work as fast as distillers' yeast, which is the powerful commercial yeast used in bakeries.
- On Day Five make up the mixture to 1½ lb, by adding 12 oz white flour and 8 oz tepid water, mixing together, covering with clingfilm, and leaving for 12–24 hours. There's no urgency since, unlike yeast, the leaven doesn't easily exhaust itself. The dough will also keep working slowly in the fridge.
- Each time you use it, keep back 8 oz to start the next batch, keeping it covered with clingfilm in a bowl in the fridge, feeding it every week with equal quantities of flour and water if not actually baking with it.

USA

California Sourdough

Long, slow maturing gives sourdough bread it's chewy texture and curious sour taste. The Forty-Niners, who in 1849 led the Gold Rush, took sourdough with them and kept back a little from each baking, to use as the 'starter' or yeast for the next batch. Craig Sams, the American who founded the wholefood business Harmony Foods, remembers the actual day he made his starter as one remembers a birthday, 14 February 1977. He makes a distinction between the true sourdough made from wholemeal flour, this one, and San Francisco sourdough made with white flour.

First you must make a sourdough starter. But once you have made this yeasty mixture, you can keep it indefinitely, but some of it should be used at least every 10 days. Each time you use some of it, replenish it with flour and water (page 157) to make up what you have removed. It will continue to work in the fridge.

SOURDOUGH STARTER

1 teaspoon dried yeast
8 fl oz warm water
4 oz wholemeal flour (freshly milled is best)

- Dissolve the yeast in the warm water and leave for 10 minutes. Slowly mix in the flour.
- Leave at room temperature for several days, but not in a cold place.
- The starter is ready when it is fermented and bubbly. The yeast will have died down and been replaced by *lacto-bacilli*.
- Stir and refrigerate.

To feed your starter When you have removed the 8 fl oz of the sourdough starter to make bread, remember to feed the remainder of the starter – ready for your next loaf. Do this by adding 1 part flour to 2 parts lukewarm water, for example, 4 oz wholemeal flour to 8 fl oz lukewarm water. Mix with the starter, stir and refrigerate until ready to use.

MAKES 2 LOAVES

1½ lb wholemeal flour
8 fl oz sourdough starter (see above)
16 fl oz warm water
1 tablespoon sea-salt
3 fl oz vegetable oil (optional)

- Mix the starter, warm water, salt and vegetable oil together. Add the flour. Knead until a dough is formed. Different kinds of flour have different degrees of water absorption – hard wheats soak up more, soft wheats less, so don't follow recipes blindly. Make a dough that has the texture that you feel is best.
- Put in a non-metallic bowl and leave to rise for 2–4 hours or until double in size.
- Form 2 loaves from the dough and place in oiled bread tins. Leave to rise for 1–3 hours or until 1½–2 times larger.
- Preheat the oven to 350°F, 180°C, gas mark 4. Bake the loaves for about 40 minutes, then cool on wire racks.

4

RICE AND GRAINS

The grain most eaten in the world is rice. It is the staple food of all the peoples of the East where the climate and growing conditions (waterlogged fields) best suit it, though there are fine varieties of rice, fat and robust, grown in the Po Valley in Italy, and near Valencia in Spain. Each country has a preferred cooking method which is appropriate to the particular style of rice.

In Japan the glutinous starch glues the rice together so you can make sushi rolls; in China bowls of sticky rice cling to the chopsticks instead of falling off; in India where many eat with their fingers the rice is washed many times to rid it of its starch so that each steamed grain is perfect, white and separate. In Italy and Spain the risottos and paellas exploit the starchiness of the grain (the rice is never washed before cooking) but a paella is not stirred during cooking, and a risotto is, the starch and stock producing a creamy coating which binds in the flavours.

In the Middle East and North Africa whole wheat grain is used like rice and cooked to absorb stocks and meat juices, but the wheat is cracked first, and sometimes partly pre-cooked, to give bulgar (in its various national spellings) and cous cous.

In parts of Africa sorghum is a grain eaten as a staple food, which we know only as bird feed. This also goes for millet, though this is mixed with rice in Korea to make the rice go farther. A similar seed is quinoa, grown by the Indians of the High Andes in South America, and added to potato soups to give added texture and nutrition. One of the most loved grains is the buckwheat (or kasha) of Eastern and northern Europe, though not strictly a grain, but the seed of a rambling member of the rhubarb family. As a flour it provides the character in blinis, as a grain it is a delicious alternative to rice or potatoes.

In Britain and America we know and love our oats (ground into medium or fine meal) or flaked, and we use barley flakes in our muesli, though the whole barley which thickened our soups is fading to a memory. All these grains add flavour and variety to the table, and we now realise they deserve our closer attention again, forming as they do the base of the Healthy Eating Pyramid.

In the Philippines there is a research station with no fewer than several thousand varieties of rice, *oryngis sativa*, the grass that grows in water. Rice is more than the staff of life in many oriental countries, it is life itself, since the communities which grow it are held together by its labour-intensive cultivation. Much changed in that respect, in the 1970s when an American-led Green Revolution produced new super grains.

Brown rice was the totem of the Zen macrobiotic movement of the 1960s, associated with flower power and hippies making love not war. 'Macrobiotic' was a name coined by a westernised Japanese, George Ohsawa, who introduced the diet of Japanese Zen Buddhists to America. Brown rice, with its seven fine skins, cooked unwashed and unhulled was the central point of the faith since it contains a perfect balance of *yin* (acid) and *yang* (alkali) in the proportions of 5 to 1, so therefore it was perfect, in the view of the Nobel Prize-winning chemist, Dr René Dubos. It would be possible to live off it, eating nothing else. However, although brown rice is indeed highly nutritious, nutritionists consider it would be dangerous to eat nothing else for any length of time.

Unpolished rice is certainly better for you, the process of polishing it strips away the useful layer of vitamin B^1 (thiamine) which protects the body against the debilitating wasting disease *beri beri*: a matter of significance if you live in a part of the world where rice is a main ingredient of the diet. When British forces were besieged in Trichinopoly in India, their Indian cooks served washed rice to the British officers, making soup from the water it was washed in to feed the Indian rank-and-file sepoys. The officers developed *beri beri*, and the Indian sepoys stayed well.

Guide to rices

Long grain or basmati From the Indes Valley in India. Light, dry and fluffy when cooked, the grains separate easily. Cook without salt to appreciate its nutty sweetness. Best when cooked in the minimum of water in its own steam.

Patna Slightly larger-grained rice, suitable for pilaffs and pillaus and the natural partner to soak up curry sauces.

American long grain rice (Such as Uncle Ben) Servicable and solid rice with not a lot of flavour of its own; fine to mop up wet casseroles, stews, curries, or as a backdrop to a highly-flavoured Cajun dish from New Orleans. Various kinds of long grain rice are used in Malaysia, Thailand, Indonesia and the Philippines and are therefore appropriate for their style of cooking.

Medium grain rice Absorbent, round grains used for risottos and paellas. In Italy the yellow-grained *cristallo* and *avorio* are the firmer, more suitable rices, though *arborio* is more easily obtainable, with its rather softer texture (in the south the cooked *arborio* is shaped into balls, stuffed with soft cheese, and deep-fried to make *arancini*).

In Spain most rice is grown in Valencia and the Marismas. The best variety, if you can get it, is from Pego (between Valencia and Alicante), where I once lived for a year, and watched it being harvested and threshed, trampled by a carousel of mules.

Sticky rice In Japan and a large part of China they use glutinous rice which is appropriate to their use of chopsticks. The Japanese wife of a friend of mine cooks rice every single day, and like every other Japanese she knows, makes it in a special rice steamer which gauges the volume of water required and precise cooking time.

Brown rice Can be any of these varieties, the difference being that it has been husked but not milled and polished. This leaves the outer skin (the bran) intact, and with it precious vitamin B^1. It needs to be brought to a fast boil, then cooked for about 40 minutes, covered and left to stand for another 10 minutes.

INDIA

Steamed Rice

The best-flavoured, plain rice to accompany any Indian dish, in my opinion, is *basmati*, sweet and nutty. If you could obtain it there is a variety which is aged for a year to develop a certain richness. Although rice is often successfully boiled in plenty of water, this process dilutes the excellent flavour (and disperses the vitamin content). In this technique, common in India, only the exact amount of water the rice needs to absorb is added. It starts as a boiling process, but as the water is absorbed the rice continues cooking in steam. If you have time this is the optimum method (but if you cut out the pre-soaking time, increase the volume of cooking water to 1½ pints).

SERVES 4

1 lb basmati rice *1⅓ pints water*

- Clean the rice carefully, rinsing it in a sieve, until no milky starch remains (or the grains will not separate as they should at the end of steaming). Leave in the saucepan, covered in water to soak and swell for 15–20 minutes. Then drain, leaving grains to sit in the sieve a further 15–20 minutes. At this stage of pre-cooking the grains are very delicate and will break up in the cooking if you don't handle them carefully.
- Place in a heavy-based pan with a tight-fitting lid, and cover with the water. Bring to the boil. Then immediately turn down the heat to its lowest. Place the tight-fitting lid on top, ensuring that no steam escapes – add a layer of crumpled kitchen foil.

- Cook for exactly 12 minutes. Then raise the heat dramatically for a few moments before turning it off. On no account lift the lid to look, but leave it to stand for at least 12 minutes more (or up to 30 minutes). The grains will be perfectly separated.
- You can induce a little more flavour by gently frying the drained rice in a little vegetable oil before adding the water, and steam-cooking as described. Don't fry basmati rice roughly or the grain will break up into small pieces.
- Patna rice is more robust, and can be cooked in the same way. But the blunderbuss technique of cooking rice, imprecise but effective, is to half cook it (5 minutes) in plenty of boiling water, drain, and finish cooking in a medium oven in a shallow dish covered with foil for about 20 minutes. Cook more than you want, because when cold it is excellent when fried (useful if you're making Chinese fried rice).

JAPAN/USA

Brown Rice

Brown rice is respected by nutritionists because it still has its outer covering of bran which provides fibre in our diet. It tastes good and is chewy.

SERVES 4

½ lb long grain brown rice
1 pint water
½ teaspoon sea-salt

- Rinse the rice, and put in a heavy-based saucepan with the water and salt. Bring to a rapid boil, cover, then turn the heat down and cook gently for 45 minutes.
- Take the saucepan off the heat and leave, still covered, for a further 5–10 minutes for the rice to continue cooking in its own heat.

ITALY

Risotto

This is the classic Italian rice dish. It is open to dozens of variations, but the one constant is that the grain is first added to oil (or butter) in the pan, and the simmering stock, which is kept on the stove to one side, is added gradually. It is cooked when still slightly chewy. It is particularly delicious made with a mixture of dried mushrooms (use the liquid you soak them in) and lightly fried chopped fresh mushrooms. You can add chopped kidney, chicken liver and peas, adding them before the rice is put in. You can also give the stock a kick by adding a glass of red or white wine.

SERVES 4

1 lb Italian short grain rice (arborio)
2 pints beef or chicken stock
1 onion, chopped
pinch of saffron
2 tablespoons grated Parmesan cheese
salt and pepper
2 tablespoons olive oil

- In a frying-pan, preferably non-stick, fry the chopped onion in olive oil until golden brown.
- Add the rice and saffron, mix well and cook until the rice starts to become transparent (a couple of minutes) stirring all the time.
- Have the stock ready on the side, at boiling point, and add gradually to the rice in small quantities, stirring continually. Season to taste.
- Cook for 18–20 minutes, stirring occasionally.
- Just before it is ready, stir in the Parmesan cheese. When ready, remove from the heat.
- Quite often Italian chefs stir in a little butter to give a shiny, glossy finish.
- Serve extra Parmesan cheese on the table with the risotto.

SPAIN

Paella

There are many dozens of rice dishes in the province of Valencia, the rice-growing region of Spain, but the one which is famous the world over is *paella*, so named because it is cooked in a wide, flat, two-handled frying pan called a *paella*. The Spanish are very strict about its exact composition, and the precise cooking method, though they accept that smart chefs in tourist spots break the rules in order to offer, and charge for, a premium product, which explains the delightful garnishes of crayfish, prawns and mussels. This is the original and authentic recipe, and how you break the rules is up to you. You are unlikely to want to include snails, and pork is a fair substitute for rabbit.

Crayfish, prawns, mussels, seafood have their place too, but the name of that dish is not paella, but *arroz marinera*. This is *paella valenciana*. If you do not have a paella pan, use a very wide frying pan, as it's essential that the rice is cooked in a shallow layer.

SERVES 4 TO 6

12 oz short grain rice (bomba or arborio)
3 pints water
1 lb corn-fed chicken, cut into pieces
1 lb rabiit, cut into pieces
16 cleaned snails (or sprig rosemary)
2 tablespoons olive oil
5 oz green beans, cut into 1 inch pieces
4 oz lima beans, soaked overnight, drained and rinsed
4 oz white butter beans, soaked overnight, drained and rinsed
4 oz tomatoes, deseeded and finely chopped
pinch saffron strands
1 tablespoon paprika
salt

- Cook the soaked, dried butter beans and lima beans in a pint of water for 45 minutes or until nearly soft.
- Trim the chicken and rabbit, leaving the bones in.
- Heat the oil in a 16 inch paella pan with a pinch of salt. When hot, fry the chicken and rabbit in it over a medium heat until golden brown on all sides.
- Add the green beans and fry for 5 minutes, then add the tomatoes and cook another 3 minutes.
- In another pan, boil the snails for 5 minutes and drain.
- Steep and crush the saffron in a little boiling water.
- Sprinkle the paprika in the pan, add the water and the rest of the beans and bring to the boil.
- Now add the snails (or the rosemary), the saffron, and another pinch of salt.
- Simmer, covered with a sheet of foil, for 30–45 minutes until the meat is tender. (If the level of the liquid has gone down, top it up with boiling water.)
- Sprinkle the rice into the boiling liquid and cook over a high heat for 10 minutes.
- Turn down the heat, and leave to cook without disturbing for 10 minutes until the liquid has evaporated.
- If it doesn't seem completely cooked at the end, don't just add more hot water, but take it off the heat and cover it with a dampened, folded tea-cloth, or even a newspaper, for 10 minutes. Left to stand, the rice will continue to cook to perfection.

ALBANIA

Sultana Pilaff

This is a national dish from a country not famous for its cuisine or for anything very much, its borders having been closed to visitors for most of the post-war years. Serve this sweetish savoury rice dish as a main course for two, or as an accompaniment to chicken.

SERVES 2 AS A MAIN COURSE

8 oz long grain rice
1 pint chicken stock
2 oz butter
4 oz sultanas
2 tablespoons sugar mixed with pinch cinnamon

- Melt the butter in a frying pan and gently cook the rice until it turns translucent.
- Stir in the stock gradually and cook for 5 minutes.
- Mix in the sultanas, cover with a lid, and cook for 15 minutes on a medium heat until all the stock is absorbed (add a little more hot liquid if the rice is still not soft).
- Before serving sprinkle with the sugar and cinnamon.

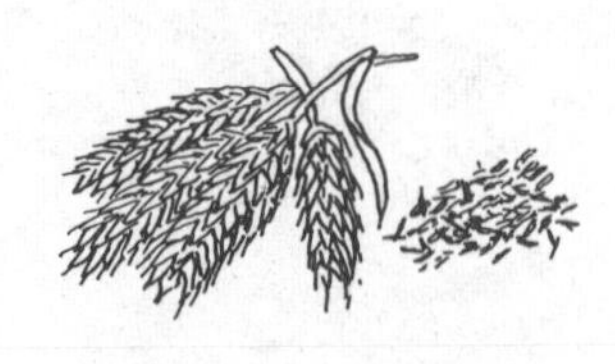

COLOMBIA

Coconut Rice

Coconut milk is delicious with both rice and fish and a common ingredient in the cooking of coastal areas in Colombia (and Brazil too). The coconut milk used in cooking is not the delicious liquid from inside the coconut which is so refreshing in summer, but a liquid made from steeping the grated fresh white flesh in boiling water. You can buy coconut milk in cans, in packets, or make your own by soaking either grated fresh or desiccated coconut in boiling water and then straining. Serve coconut rice with a main dish, such as spicy hot fish.

SERVES 4

1¼ pints coconut milk
4 oz raisins
6 oz long grain rice
1 teaspoon sugar
pinch salt

- Put the rice, raisins, sugar and salt in a large saucepan and bring to the boil.
- Cover, lower the heat (preferably use a diffusing mat) and cook for about 20–25 minutes, till the rice is soft.

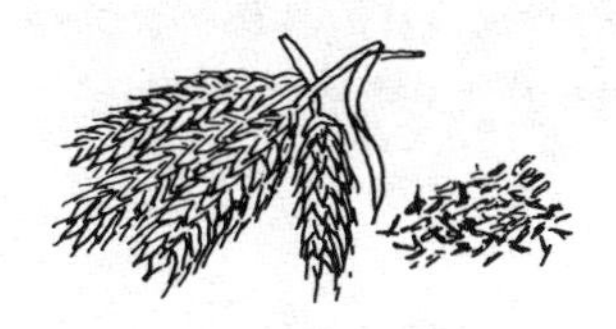

GUATEMALA

Rice and Vegetables
Arroz Guatemalco

A typical, appealing rice dish from Central America where meat and fish may be at a premium, but the varied vegetables create an appetising meal. It is, in effect, a vegetarian risotto.

SERVES 4

8 oz long grain rice
2 tablespoons peanut oil
1 small onion, chopped
1 tomato, skinned and chopped
1 clove garlic, peeled and chopped
½ lb chopped mixed vegetables (such as carrots, peas, green peppers, celery)
salt and pepper
several sprigs fresh coriander chopped, as a garnish

- Wash the rice thoroughly.
- Heat the oil in a heavy casserole, add the rice and fry, stirring constantly until golden.
- Add the remaining ingredients except the coriander, bring to the boil, cover and simmer over a low heat without stirring until all the liquid has been absorbed and the rice is tender (about 20 minutes). Add more water if necessary.
- Garnish with coriander.

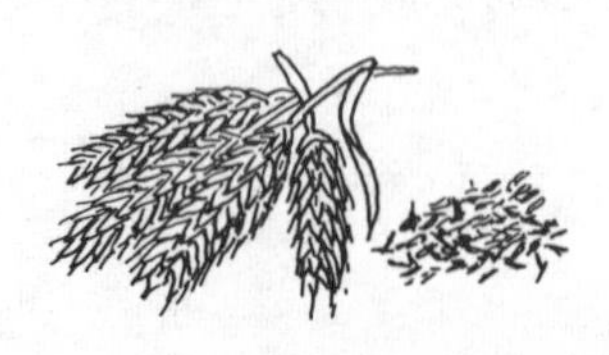

PORTUGAL

Rice with Spring Greens

This economical rice dish suits the cold, wet Atlantic coast, being made with turnip tops, Brussels sprout tops or spring greens and the typical European root vegetables of carrot, potato and onion. The Portuguese wouldn't use the Dutch white cabbage, as it lacks the necessary bite and flavour.

SERVES 4

½ lb long grain rice
½ lb spring greens, turnip tops or Brussels sprout tops
1 pint chicken stock
1 onion, sliced
2 carrots, sliced thinly
1 potato, peeled and diced
2 cloves garlic, peeled and chopped
5 tablespoons olive oil

- Heat half the oil in a heavy, large saucepan, and sweat the onion, carrots and potato gently for about 5 minutes.
- Add the rice and stir well in the oil. Cook for another 5 minutes, stirring to prevent burning.
- Add the boiling stock, cover the pan and simmer for about 20 minutes, or until the stock is absorbed and the rice tender.
- In another saucepan, heat the rest of the oil, cook the garlic without letting it burn and then add the turnip tops. Toss them well then add a little water and salt, and cover the pan.
- Cook for 5–10 minutes, till soft.
- Drain and stir into the rice mixture.

ENGLAND

Kedgeree

A satisfying breakfast or brunch dish combining rice and smoked haddock. It is assumed that it is an Anglo-Indian dish because it contains curry and rice, though the Indian dish, *khichiree,* is actually rice and lentils.

SERVES 4

1 lb smoked haddock
1 pint milk and water (half and half)
1 bay leaf
8 oz Patna or basmati long grain rice
2 hard-boiled eggs
1 onion, finely sliced
1 tablespoon vegetable oil
1 heaped teaspoon good curry powder (or your own mixture of ground cumin, coriander, turmeric, ginger, fenugreek, cinnamon, chilli pepper)
1 teaspoon cornflour
sprig parsley or green coriander, chopped

- Poach the haddock in the milk and water in a covered frying pan with a bay leaf.
- When cool enough to handle, flake the fish, removing the bones.
- Rinse the rice in several changes of water till it runs clear, then cook till soft, about 12 minutes, drain, cover and keep warm.
- Fry the onion in hot oil till soft and slightly coloured, then add the spices and cook for several minutes, stirring, to get rid of their sharp, raw flavours.
- Dissolve the cornflour in a little cold milk, add to the onions, and then stir enough of the poaching liquid to make a thin, creamy sauce. Let it simmer a few moments, covered with a lid, to absorb the flavours. Check the seasoning.
- Mix the smoked haddock with the rice, arrange the quartered hard-boiled eggs on top, and pour the curry sauce over.

USA

Jambalaya

Rich sticky, glutinous rice dish invented by the first French settlers in New Orleans, where freshwater crayfish abound. The word *jambon* is French for 'ham'.

SERVES 6

8 oz long grain rice
½ lb smoked bacon or ham (or smoked sausage) cut into ½ inch squares
¾ lb peeled prawns (or 6 raw crayfish or king prawns)
1 green pepper, deseeded and diced
1 onion, chopped
1 green chilli, deseeded
¾ pint water (or chicken stock)
14 oz can tomatoes
1 tablespoon plain flour
2 tablespoons oil (or butter or, traditionally, bacon fat)
2 cloves garlic
pinch thyme
salt, pepper, cayenne
sprig parsley, chopped

- Cook the onion and smoked ham (or sausage) in the oil (or butter or bacon fat) in a frying pan covered with a lid.
- Remove the lid, add the flour and cook till it browns slightly.
- Add the garlic and stir in, and then the tomatoes, thyme, chilli, green pepper, salt, pepper and cayenne. Remove from the heat.
- In a separate pan simmer the rice in the water (or stock) until half-cooked (about 10 minutes).
- Mix together the tomato mixture and rice. Cover and cook in the oven for 1–1¼ hours at 350°F, 180°C, gas mark 4, or until the liquid is completely absorbed.
- Alternatively, cook on the top of the stove on a diffuser mat on low heat for 25–30 minutes or until the liquid is absorbed.
- Add the raw or cooked prawns during the last few minutes.
- Sprinkle with the parsley and serve very hot.

JAPAN

Sushi

Sushi is the snack bar food of Japan, but unlike Western junk food, is a delicacy which is often extremely expensive. Those who prepare it so skilfully will have trained for a good three years, so be tolerant to yourself if your first efforts don't have quite the elegance you'd hoped for. The Chef des Cuisines of the Savoy, Anton Edelman, makes sushi at home as appetisers before Sunday drinks if he's having friends round, and not just as a novelty, as they are delicious, exciting and stimulate the appetite. The fish must be as fresh out of the sea as possible, so explain to your amazed fishmonger that you do plan to eat it raw. It's also important to get Japanese rice which is different in texture to Western rices.

SERVES 4 TO 6

8 oz Japanese short grain rice (ask for 'sticky rice')
water, measured to equal volume
4 tablespoons rice vinegar
1 tablespoon sugar
1 teaspoon salt
raw fish to taste, for example, 4 oz each salmon, turbot, scallops, calamari, langoustine (soak in iced water for 2 hours to produce a silky texture)
wasabi powder, made into mustard
Japanese radish (daikon) peeled, and finely sliced
packet pickled Japanese ginger slices
1 oz sesame seeds, toasted
soy sauce for dipping (Kikkoman is best brand)

- Wash the rice in several changes of water till it runs clear and leave in a sieve to drain for 1 hour.
- Put the rice and an equal volume of water in a pan with a close-fitting lid, bring to boil, and lower the heat, cooking for 16 minutes, till the water is absorbed. But don't lift the lid to check.
- Turn the heat up to high for 10 seconds. Then remove the rice from the heat completely, and leave to stand, still covered, for 15 minutes longer.
- Heat the vinegar, sugar and salt.
- Turn the rice into a shallow bowl and with a wooden spatula stir in the vinegar mixture, fanning to cool it as you go. You can make the sushi as soon as it's cool, using a bowl with vinegary water in it to rinse your hands. The mixture will keep for hours if you cover it with a cloth.
- Spread a ¼ inch thick layer of rice on to a bamboo place mat about 8 inches square.
- Carefully arrange your chosen ingredients in a line across the middle.
- Roll the mat away from you, making one or two turns to produce a cylinder shape. Squeeze gently to firm it up.
- Rest for 5 minutes and then unroll and cut across into 6 strips, revealing the attractive colours inside.
- Serve with more wasabi mustard on top, and a soy sauce for dipping.

INDONESIA

Nasi Goreng

Rice is the staple food of Indonesia, but such are the Indonesians' cooking skills that every dish is a feast. The rice should be cooked the day before.

SERVES 4

1 lb long grain rice (Patna or basmati) cooked, and left to cool
½ oz butter
4 oz raw chicken, diced
4 oz peeled prawns
6 oz French beans
2 cloves garlic, crushed and chopped
2 dried red chillies, crumbled, or ½ teaspoon cayenne
salt and pepper
vegetable oil

For the garnish
1 onion, sliced and fried quickly in hot oil, till brown
1 egg, beaten, made into thin omelette, rolled and sliced
few leaves iceberg lettuce

- In a large pan (a wok is ideal), fry the garlic in a little oil.
- Toss in the chilli (or cayenne) with the prawns, chicken, beans and seasoning and stir-fry for about 3 minutes.
- Lower the heat, and toss in the cold rice, stirring and blending.
- When steaming hot, serve garnished with caramelised onion slices, omelette shreds and lettuce.

CANADA

Mushroom and Wild Rice Casserole

It's not true to say that the expensive, hand-harvested, long skinny black grains of wild rice are the caviar of the rice family – not gastronomically, although the grains have a nutty, chewy character, and certainly not botanically, since this aquatic wild grass from Canada is not of the rice family. However it is attractive with game dishes, in stuffings, or as a garnish, mixed with a dish of plain rice.

SERVES 4

6 oz wild rice
12 oz mushrooms, sliced
1 medium onion, finely sliced
2 oz butter
1½ pints beef stock
pinch thyme
sprig basil
pinch salt
salt and pepper

- Rinse the rice under running water. Put it in a heavy saucepan with the stock and herbs, cover tightly and bring to the boil, then simmer over a low heat for about 45 minutes.
- On the stove, gently fry the onions for 5 minutes till soft but not coloured, then stir in the sliced mushrooms and cook until they change colour.
- Combine the mushrooms, onion and rice (which should have absorbed most of the stock) in an oiled, 3 pint casserole and season with salt and pepper to taste.
- Bake in a moderate oven (350°F, 180°C, gas mark 4) for 15–20 minutes.

KOREA

Five Grain Rice

Millet isn't a grain we have a great dependency upon and most people aren't prepared to include birdseed in their diet. Vegetarians however, appreciate its value in adding a crunchy texture to bread, soups and vegetable stews. In some parts of the world it plays an essential role in stretching the nutritional value of other grains. In Korea, when rice is scarce and expensive, this solid meal is served.

SERVES 4

4 oz long grain rice
2 oz millet
2 oz pearl barley
2 oz black beans
2 oz red kidney beans

- Soak the red and black beans overnight, after boiling them for 10 minutes to remove the toxins.
- Soak the barley and the millet for 2 hours.
- Cook the beans in plenty of water until they are tender, (1–1½ hours). Reserve the cooking liquid for use later.
- Rinse the rice till the water runs clear, and mix it well with the beans, the pearl barley and the millet. Cover with 1½ pints water, including the liquid used to cook the beans. Bring to the boil, cover tightly and turn the heat down to low. Let the contents of the pan cook in their own steam for 30 minutes.
- Another way is to use millet to add texture and flavour to otherwise plain boiled rice is to rinse the rice well, and wash and drain the millet, then combine them both and put into a medium-sized saucepan with twice the volume of water. Bring to the boil, cover tightly, reduce the heat to low and cook the grains in their own steam for 25–30 minutes. Don't lift the lid while they are cooking.

RUSSIA

Kasha

Buckwheat, known in Russia as *kasha*, is not in fact a grain, but the seed of a rambling rhubarb plant with fleshy leaves like a nasturtium. It grows in northern Europe in climates hostile to wheat, so its use is forced on these people by necessity rather than choice. The whole buckwheat grain is delicious covered with stock as a starchy accompaniment to meat, or like a pilaff or risotto, as a dish in its own right (see page 180). If you buy unroasted buckwheat, which is yellowy grey, you need to roast it or 'toast' it to a golden mahogany colour in order to cook it.

SERVES 4

1 lb buckwheat
2 tablespoons oil or 2 oz butter
stock (or water)
1 teaspoon salt

- Roast the buckwheat in an ungreased frying pan, stirring so that the grains do not burn, until the grains are a pale golden colour.
- Put in an ovenproof dish, season with salt, stir in the oil (or butter) and pour on enough boiling water to cover.
- Bake in a slow oven, 300°F, 150°C, gas mark 2, for 2½ hours.

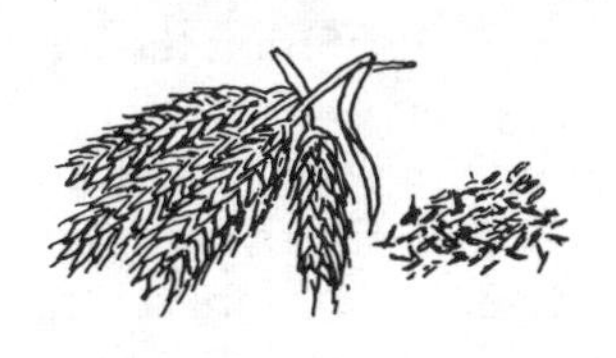

POLAND

Kasha and Mushroom Sauce

Kasha, whole buckwheat grain, available in health food stores, is a staple food in Poland, as common in their cooking as risotto is in Italy, which this dish resembles in character. It is often eaten with a bowl of chilled, sour milk, like yoghurt. This is prepared the day before. To make it, pour a pint of warmed milk into a basin and stir in 2 tablespoons of live yoghurt. Cover with a tea-cloth and keep in a warm place to set overnight. Chill for a while before eating.

SERVES 4

1 lb toasted buckwheat (untoasted buckwheat is mushy)
16 fl oz lukewarm water
salt
½ onion, finely chopped
1 small packed dried ceps or porcini
1 oz butter
1 oz flour
¼ pint meat stock
dill as garnish (if you can get it)

- Pour a little boiling water on to the dried ceps in a cup and soak for 30 minutes or so.
- Chop the mushrooms finely. Strain the liquid through a sieve to remove any grit, and reserve.
- Cover the buckwheat with warm water and salt and bring to the boil. Lower the heat, cover tightly and cook for 12 minutes.
- Fry the onions gently in butter until soft and yellow.
- Stir in the flour, then slowly add the stock and liquid from the mushrooms, stirring for 10 minutes.
- Pour over the kasha and serve.

TURKEY

Bulgur Salad
Tabbouleh

This is an appetising, refreshing, nourishing summer salad. I've had a particularly delicious version in which the grains have been soaked overnight not in water but tomato juice. A less precise way of preparing the bulgur is to stand the grains in a bowl covered with water for 15 minutes, and then squeeze the water out of the bulgur (between your fingers).

SERVES 4

6 oz bulgur or cracked wheat
¼ pint water, lukewarm
6–8 spring onions, finely chopped
1 lb ripe tomatoes, skinned, chopped
½ green pepper, deseeded, chopped
handful parsley, finely chopped
juice ½ lemon
3 tablespoons olive oil
1 teaspoon salt

- Put the bulgur in a bowl with the salt and pour over the water. Cover and leave for 15 minutes.
- With a wooden spoon, mix the onion well, then the oil, lemon juice, tomatoes, green pepper and parsley. Add more salt if necessary. Chill for at least half an hour.

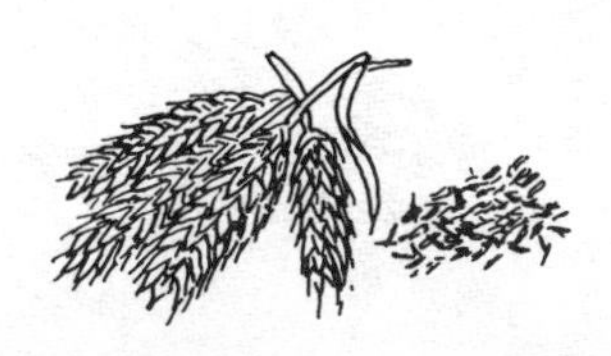

TURKEY

Bulgur Pilaff

Bulgur in Turkey, *bulgar* in Bulgaria, of course, and *pourgouri* in Greece are all forms of the same grain, hulled wheat, broken up into varying degrees of coarseness and fineness. It's often sold in wholefood stores as cracked wheat. This dish is to Turkey what risotto is to Italy.

SERVES 4

½ lb bulgur
2 tablespoons oil (or butter)
1 onion, finely chopped
1 green pepper, deseeded, sliced
1 × 14 oz can tomatoes
¾ pint chicken or lamb stock
2 oz pine nuts or blanched almonds, chopped
1 oz sultanas
salt and pepper

- Fry the onion in the oil (or butter) till soft, but not browned.
- Add the green pepper and cook for a few minutes more.
- Stir in the bulgur, and cook a few minutes until the oil is absorbed.
- Add the tomatoes.
- Finally add the stock and bring to the boil.
- Add the seasonings, nuts and sultanas. Turn down the heat, and cook for 10–15 minutes until the stock has been absorbed.
- Cover tightly, seal with foil if necessary, and stand on the lowest heat on a diffuser, and leave to cook in its own steam for another 15–20 minutes.

MOROCCO

Chicken Cous Cous

A Cous Cous Royale is a mixture of lamb (mutton really) and chicken (a cockerel rather than a supermarket broiler) providing a rich stock and great depth of flavour, to which a wide variety of vegetables add texture and supply colour (green, white, red, orange and yellow, from red peppers, carrot and pumpkin). This dish is based on the Seven-Vegetable Cous Cous from Fez.

SERVES 4 TO 6

1 chicken, cut into 8
2 large onions, quartered
4 carrots, scraped and quartered
2 or 3 green chillies (optional), pierced, not sliced
bundle green herbs, including coriander if possible
stick cinnamon
1 oz butter and 1 tablespoon olive oil
½ teaspoon turmeric
salt and freshly ground pepper
pinch saffron
3 pints water (or chicken stock)
8 oz chickpeas (soak overnight, cook 1 hour, rub off skins in cold water), or a can of chickpeas (but add them for last half-hour of cooking only)
seven vegetables (mixed vegetables cut roughly to bite-sized pieces: 2 onions, 2 green peppers, 2 turnips, 3 carrots, 3 courgettes, 6 oz pumpkin, 1 lb tomatoes (deseeded) or can of tomatoes)

- In a heavy iron pan, melt the butter with the oil, and lightly brown the chicken pieces.
- Add the rest of the ingredients, cover and cook over a low heat for 10 minutes.
- Then add the water, bring to the boil, lower the heat and simmer for 1 hour. This can be done the night before.
- Skim off the fat and cook for another 30 minutes, adding the vegetables according to the time they take to cook, carrots first, pumpkin and tomatoes last.
- To serve, pour some of the stew on to a mound of steaming cous cous, and the remainder into a casserole dish.
- Serve with harissa sauce (see the next recipe).

MOROCCO

Harissa Sauce

Serve this on the side, leaving your guests to take a little at a time, if they are not used to it. Add more paste and stock according to your own taste.

SERVES 4 TO 6

1 teaspoon harissa paste (see page 252)
juice ½ lemon
1 tablespoon olive oil
½ pint broth from cous cous stew
leaf coriander or parsley, chopped

- Heat the ingredients together in a pan and serve sprinkled with the coriander or parsley leaves.

SWITZERLAND

Muesli

'Maslin', a mixture of grains soaked and cooked together, was known in Tudor times in England but it was tne Swiss food reformer, Dr Max Bircher-Benner, who in the 1920s put *muesli* (a word from the same etymology) on the map. In his clinic in Basle he advised his patients to increase consumption of fruit and raw vegetables, a revolutionary notion at the time among the well-to-do. It was only the poor peasants who, out of necessity, ate crushed fruit and grains and barley flakes softened overnight in water or milk, as a filling first meal of the day. This was indeed the breakfast dish among peasants in the mountains around Basle in Bircher-Benner's day. The oversweet, modern supermarket muesli bears scant relationship to his original concept. Not everyone, however, wants such a chewy muesli as the original. This mixture, made with rolled oats, doesn't need pre-soaking. This mixture is made in the spirit of Dr Max, and makes nearly 7 lb. Buy the ingredients from a good wholefood store with a fast turnover. Keep it in an airtight container.

MAKES 6½ LB

2 lb rolled oats
½ lb wheat flakes
½ lb rye flakes
½ lb barley flakes
2 lb dried fruit (raisins, sultanas, chopped dried apricots, dried dates)
1 lb nuts (almonds, hazelnuts, cashews, sunflower seeds – not peanuts)

- Blend all the ingredients and store in an airtight container. (Vary the mixture to suit your taste.)
- Serve with full-cream or skimmed milk, sour cream, yoghurt or fruit juice (apple juice is good).
- Add honey or Barbados sugar, grated or sliced fresh fruit, such as apples, pears, peaches, nectarines, apricots, bananas, orange segments, berries, and freshly toasted nuts or oatmeal.

USA

Granola

The Quakers in America were a force for food reform, and gave the impetus for most of the modern breakfast cereals eaten today, which have come a long way from the wholesome and nutritious balance of the original grain mixtures. Granola was invented by the Seventh Day Adventists and was, in fact, America's answer to muesli. The brown sugar adds sweetness, the various seeds provide a power-pack of essential vitamins. Desiccated coconut is often added, but if not fresh it gives a soapy taste. Serve with skimmed milk, and perhaps a blob of honey.

MAKES 2¼ LB

1 lb rolled oats
4 oz sesame seeds, ground
4 oz sunflower seeds, ground
4 oz pumpkin seeds, ground
4 oz brown sugar
4 oz slivered almonds
1 teaspoon sea-salt
½ teaspoon ground anise seed (if liked)

- Toast the oats for a few minutes in batches in a dry frying pan or on a baking sheet in a hot oven to brown them lightly.
- Mix with all the other ingredients, and store in jars or bags.

SCOTLAND

Porridge

Oats are back in favour ever since they were discovered to reduce cholesterol. Some centuries have passed since Scottish students would come to a London lodging with a sack of oatmeal for sustenance. In the harsher climes of parts of Scotland oats is the only cereal which grows, and it's deeply ingrained into their cooking culture. Porridge oats sold in most supermarkets are processed, rolled oats, quick to cook but lacking the satisfying texture of the oatmeal, which can be bought fine, medium or large (pinhead).

SERVES 2

⅔ oz pinhead oats	*tiny pinch salt*
1 pint water	

- Soaking the oats overnight reduces the cooking time and produces smoother porridge but it's not essential.
- Use a non-stick saucepan if you can, and stir in the oats with a wooden spoon as you bring them to simmering point.
- Turn the heat low (use a diffusing mat) and cook for 5–15 minutes, stirring occasionally. If it gets too thick it is easily thinned by stirring in a little boiling water. Serve the Scottish way with a pinch of salt and nothing more, or the English way with a little milk and a spoonful of honey.
- This produces a thick, nutty, solid textured porridge. A smoother, quicker porridge, also very good can be made with medium oatmeal (not to be confused with rolled oats): allow 5–10 minutes cooking time.

SCOTLAND
Oatcakes

Once eaten with a good, sharp, dry cheese, such as Cheshire or White Stilton, the taste and texture of home-made oatcakes become addictive. Traditionally they were made with the fat which came most readily to hand, the contents of the frying pan after cooking bacon, but sunflower oil makes an excellent, delicate biscuit.

MAKES ROUGHLY 20 OATCAKES

1 lb medium oatmeal
½–¾ pint boiling water
2 tablespoons sunflower oil (or melted bacon fat or lard)
½ teaspoon baking powder
1 heaped teaspoon salt
fine oatmeal, for rolling out

- Mix the baking powder and salt into the oatmeal.
- Mix the oil (or bacon fat) in a little of the boiling water and blend into the medium oatmeal, gradually adding just enough water to make a soft dough.
- On a board dusted with fine oatmeal, roll out as thinly as possible. The edges break up, but simply press them back into place. Use a glass to cut out circles or cut into triangles.
- Bake the oatcakes on a greased baking sheet on the top shelf of a hot oven, 425°F, 220°C, gas mark 7, for 5–10 minutes, then leave them in the oven to dry out, with the door open.
- More traditionally, they are cooked on a greased griddle (use an electric hotplate turned low) and cooked for about 5 minutes, or until the edges start to curl.

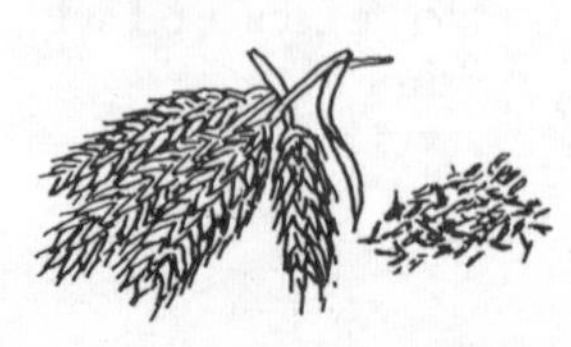

WALES

Barley Cakes

When barley was a staple crop it was not only used in breads and to add substance to broths (pearl barley), but in Wales it was made into thin griddle cakes, which turn out rather like a moist chapati with a farmyard flavour. It was traditionally cooked on a bakestone. You can buy barley meal in wholefood shops.

MAKES 6 TO 8

4 oz barley meal
10 fl oz skimmed milk
salt

- Mix the meal with enough milk to make a batter the consistency of thick cream.
- Pour it on to a hot, oiled baking sheet and bake at 300°F, 150°C, gas mark 2, for 10–15 minutes. (It is done when it is the texture of a stiff pancake.)
- You can also cook it in a frying pan or on an oiled griddle, turning to cook each side.
- Eat cold with Welsh butter or Flora.

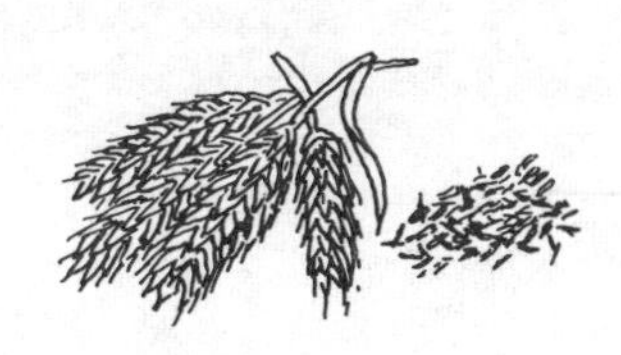

5

FISH, MEAT AND DAIRY FOODS

A diet of steaks, roasts, chops, hams, sausages and fried bacon every day, every week, is no longer a sensible way to eat, but there's no reason why we shouldn't indulge ourselves from time to time for the sheer, immense pleasure of the rich flavour that good-flavoured fat contributes to the taste of a dish.

But this is a collection of recipes from people who, for the most part, don't eat in this fashion (such as the rancheros and gauchos of Argentina and the sheep farmers of New Zealand who eat their meat off the hoof). In countries where large farm animals do not graze, what little meat is available is cut into tiny pieces and served to add nutrition and flavour to the bulk of the main meal, as in spaghetti with a long-simmered meat ragú, or a Chinese stir-fry.

This brief section, therefore, includes only a few meat and chicken dishes (though meat and chicken appear in recipes throughout other sections) but instead offers a taste of the varied ways fish is served around the world – raw, marinated, steamed, baked and stir-fried – and blended into fish cakes.

Fish

Fish is the good news story of our times. It's loved by chefs because it is a challenge to their skill, and it's everything a modern food ought to be, nutritious and wholesome in every way. All its calories are the right calories, in the form of highly-digestible, body-building protein, and it contains vitamins, minerals, phosphorous and iodine.

There are other bonuses, especially with the family of so-called oily fish, salmon, mackerel, herring, sardines and anchovies. All fish are high in polyunsaturated fats which protect the heart against blood-clotting, but most especially the oily fish which contains two essential so-called 'omega-3' fatty acids.

Fish and chips is by no means a poor form of nutrition, since the fat seals the batter and the fish steam-cooks inside a sealed envelope; the chips absorb more fat, but if cooked in unsaturated fat they are not a health risk, though the calorie count is high for fried chips.

Steamed fish may sound disgusting, but not when performed by the Chinese who add some hot oil as a final seasoning; and raw fish, and marinated fish, and pickled fish, and soused fish may be unfamiliar techniques. Certainly the world's best-loved fish dish (apart from a whole, grilled sea bass, sole or turbot) is a fish stew and the fishermen of every country in the world compete too outdo each other in this speciality.

Meat

Beef is excellent protein; it is how you use it which is significant. Half a pound of steak fried, with chips, fried onions and fried tomatoes produces a 1,000 calorie dish; grilled, the same ingredients contribute only 650 calories; halve the amount of meat, and make a stew of onions, mushrooms, tomatoes and potatoes, carrots and peas, and you reduce the calorie content of a serving to around 350 calories. The same goes for lamb and pork and even chicken, though the fat in chicken is mostly in the skin and that's easily removed, if you wish.

Animal fat is not completely saturated; about half the fat is a mixture of mono-unsaturated and unsaturated fat. Of all the animal and dairy fats, butter and cheese has the highest average of saturated fats, over 60%. Lamb is the highest animal fat, at 54%, saturated, beef next at 48%, then pork at 36%, liver at 34%, eggs at 33% and chicken at 32%. There's a dramatic drop when it comes to fish oils: the fat in herring is only 19% saturated and it has a very healthy 66% unsaturated fat.

Animals in the wild have a smaller proportion of fat than farmed animals that are intensively fed and get little exercise. In animals in the wild, the proportion of lean meat is 75% of the animal and the fat is 4%. In farmed animals, the lean meat represents 50% and the fat 25%. As fat generates more calories than the lean meat protein, the difference between a wild and farmed animal is even more dramatic. Measured in calories, the farmed animal produces ten times more calories from its fat content than a wild animal and its fat we don't want, since the main object of eating meat is to benefit from its protein value. The more intensively reared animals are, the less good they are for us.

British beef has been given a clean bill of health by the government in the aftermath of 'mad cow disease' which broke out in the 1980s. Not all food scientists are satisfied that Bovine Spongiform Encephalopathy (BSE) no longer poses a threat. Some years on, 500 cows are still being slaughtered every week and it could be some years before the disease is checked. There is no evidence that the disease can be passed to humans, but BSE seems to have passed from sheep to cows (processed sheep's brains being included in their protein feed). The government has brought in strict regulations governing the feed given to cows and in slaughterhouses they now remove and destroy the heads of the cows and their nervous tissue, hopefully extinguishing the danger to humans.

Is there anything the consumer can do? Certainly. Don't eat cow's meat. Although this is not an advertised fact, 80% of all 'beef' eaten in Britain comes from cows. The difference between a bull and a cow is more than a matter of gender. Bulls (or heifers) bred solely for meat (premium beef from the Charollais strain and Angus herds) are killed at 15 to 18 months. There is no case of any animal of this age developing BSE, so you can regard this meat as safe. Cows, on the other hand, are taken from the nation's dairy herd, and when they have exhausted their milking duties, at about the age of eight, they go to the slaughterhouse for meat.

These are the animals which have to be destroyed as soon as they develop BSE symptoms. The meat from unaffected cows goes to make meat pies, canned steak and burgers and if you want to avoid it, you must ask your butcher what he is selling. It is a little harder to know which type of meat is used when you are buying high street burgers. One burger chain makes a point of using Irish beef which has no record of BSE.

Dairy foods

Dairy foods have an important place in the diet of Northern Europe, but over-indulgence and excess in eating cheese, butter, cream and eggs is a sure route to an early coronary. One-in-three deaths among people over 35 could be postponed if fat in the diet were reduced to, at the most, 30% of the daily calorie intake.

Take 2,500 calories as the average calorie requirement for a male with a non-active office job, and 1,700 for a woman in a similar position, and you will see how quickly dairy fats can take over. What is 1,700 calories in terms of fat? Very roughly, it's a day in which you consumed 2 fried eggs, 1 pint of milk, 4 oz cheese, 4 oz cream, and 2 oz butter.

Dairy foods are so delicious, especially the finest cheeses, dairy butter, good cream and freshly-laid eggs, it would be a monastic act of self-denial to forego any of them. In any case, this is not necessary. All that is required is to treat them as luxuries, eat them often and freely but in very small quantities to savour the quality, and never to excess.

Parmesan cheese is an excellent example and its worth

buying the very best from an Italian shop in the piece (not already grated and in packets) and using it with discretion. Although the fat content is extremely high (2,080 calories to the pound), you can freshly grate a mere 2 oz to serve with spaghetti for 4 people, and each person gets the benefit of its delicious flavour yet consumes only 60 calories of fat with their pasta. Small amounts of cheese combined with pasta, pizza and potatoes add a quality of seasoning and digestibility – and increase nutritional value (about one-third of the calories in cheese are protein) with adding an undue volume of fat.

Cream is frankly a luxury to be used sparingly but certainly not never. Creaminess is a desirable texture in food, and especially in sauces, but this can be achieved by using a low-fat substitute like fromage frais, which has almost no fat at all, or plain yoghurt. If you enjoy excellent food, cream is often an ingredient, so it makes sense to enjoy cream sometimes, in small amounts, than to say never, ever again.

CHILE

Ceviche

Ceviche is raw fish that has been marinated in lime or lemon juice, a process which turns it opaque and effectively cooks it. The texture remains springy. It is enjoyed throughout Latin America, usually dressed with chopped onions, green chillies, and sometimes skinned, deseeded tomatoes. Typical of South America it may seem, but it was brought by the Spanish, who'd learnt it from Mediterranean traders who brought the practice of pickling meat in vinegar from Persia and the Arab world.

Pickled herrings are a Baltic form of ceviche, the pickle being a cooked vinegar marinade. Some modern English restaurants serve a version which they choose to call a *carpaccio*, flattening fleshy fish such as monk fish with a mallet, serving it dressed with lime juice and served with salad leaves.

SERVES 4

1 lb fillet good, white, fresh fish
juice 2 limes (or lemon)
1 Spanish onion, finely chopped
2 green chillies, deseeded, finely chopped (or 2 dry red chilli peppers, crumbled)
1 clove garlic, crushed, finely chopped

- Remove the skin and the bones of fish, and cut it into 1 inch squares.
- Mix the marinade ingredients in a bowl, and toss the pieces of the fish in the mixture until well coated. Leave for at least 30 minutes, or up to 2 hours, to 'cook'. Serve with a salad and good bread.

SWEDEN

Soused Herring

Oily fish contain omega oils, which lower cholesterol and decrease the likelihood of heart disease, but if you don't like the rich flavour of mackerel, herring and sardines, you'd do better taking a cod liver oil tablet before breakfast every day.

Curing fish (salting and smoking) transforms its fatty character, and smoked salmon and kippered herrings hardly taste like the fresh fish. But fish cooked in vinegar (similar in style to a ceviche, see page 196) provides an equally amazing transformation. The Norwegians, Danes and Swedes all have recipes for soused mackerel and herring.

SERVES 4

4 small herrings (or 2 mackerels)
1 onion, sliced in rings
½ pint white wine vinegar
½ pint water
12 peppercorns
1 bay leaf

- Ask your fishmonger to clean the fish, and open them and remove the back bone.
- Spread the fish out in an oven dish, cover with the vinegar and water mixture, scatter with the onions and add the bay leaf and peppercorns.
- Bake in moderate oven, 350°F, 180°C, gas mark 4, for 15 minutes.
- Leave to cool in the marinade mixture. Leave the fish for a day, if in the fridge, covered with clingfilm.
- Eat with good bread.

SWEDEN

Gravad Lax

Lax means 'salmon'; *gravad* means 'buried' (as in grave), in this case under a weight, and pickled in sugar, which acts hydroscopically to complement the salt in drawing out moisture, the role played by salt in the curing of salmon before smoking. The sweetness of the sugar, the sensational aniseed flavour of dill, the oiliness of the fish, and the mustardy dressing contribute to a unique taste sensation. Serve with mustard sauce, freshly made toast and butter, lager and a cold schnapps, or if you prefer it, a dry white wine.

SERVES 6

2 lb fresh salmon, middlecut if possible
2 oz caster sugar
large bunch fresh dill
2 oz coarse salt
10 peppercorns, crushed

- Scrape and dry the salmon, but do not wash it. Halve it along the backbone and remove this and any other bones, picking out the 'pin-bones' with tweezers or pliers.
- Mix the sugar and salt, and rub the fish on all sides with the mixture.
- Make a bed of some of the dill in a shallow dish and place half of the salmon on top, skin down. Sprinkle with more dill and the peppercorns.
- Place the other piece of salmon, skin uppermost, on top and cover with more dill.
- Cover with a conveniently sized piece of wood, or chopping board, and put a heavy weight on top to press the salmon firmly together. Keep in a cool, dark place for at least 48 hours. It will keep for a week if kept cold.

- Arrange the salmon on a wooden board, decorate with sprigs of dill and carve in not-too-thin slices, discarding the skin. Serve with mustard dressing (see next recipe).

MUSTARD DRESSING

2 tablespoons German mustard (mild)
1 egg yolk
tablespoon sunflower or groundnut oil
2 tablespoons vinegar
1 tablespoon sugar
chopped dill
salt and pepper

- Mix the mustard, sugar, vinegar and egg yolk in a bowl. Add the oil slowly, whisking all the time until well blended. Add the dill, season with salt and pepper and keep cool in an airtight container.

AUSTRALIA

Shellfish Soup with Lobster Wontons

Until 10 years ago the national dish of Australia was meat pie, sauce and peas, and cooking was still based on the meat and potatoes ethos the first settlers brought with them. But modern Australian restaurants started to create a new cooking style embracing their neighbours on the Pacific Rim. This recipe was given to me by Gay Bilson, whose restaurant, Berowra Waters (north of Sydney), was one of the true pioneers of the new cuisine.

SERVES 4

wonton skins (from a Chinese store)
½ lb shellfish (lobster or prawns)
1 inch fresh ginger root
4–6 spring onions
pinch saffron
salt and pepper

For the fish stock

2 lb fish heads and bones of good white fish (turbot, sole, conger, etc)
½ onion
white of leek
2 oz mushrooms
2 oz butter
2 glasses dry white wine
piece dried orange peel
stick vanilla
bouquet garni (green of leek, thyme, parsley, bayleaf)
4 pints water

For the soup

2 pints fish stock
2 tomatoes, chopped
1 carrot, grated
stick celery, finely cut
white of leek, sliced
shell and heads of lobster (or prawns) crushed up
pinch of saffron

- Make the stock by first soaking the fish bones and heads for 3 hours in cold water. Sweat the vegetables in the butter, but don't brown.
- Add the bones (chopped up), heat through, then add the wine. Reduce on a fierce heat, then cover with the water, bring to the boil and skim well.
- Add the bouquet garni, orange peel and vanilla, and simmer for 25 minutes. Strain.
- Simmer all the ingredients for the soup, except the saffron, for 20 minutes.
- Strain through a sieve.
- Put the saffron in a cup with a little boiling water. Crush with back of spoon and leave for 10 minutes to infuse. Then add it to the soup.
- Chop the shellfish small and mix with finely chopped spring onion and ginger juice (use garlic press).
- Place a teaspoon of chopped shellfish on each wonton skin, fold together and seal.
- Poach the wontons in the soup for just 3 minutes and serve.

FRANCE

Classic French Fish Soup

Soupe de Poissons with Rouille

Peasants don't have a monopoly of all the healthy dishes of the world, as this elegant fish soup shows. Vary the ingredients according to what is available.

SERVES 4

2 red mullet, 6 oz each
1 sea bass, 1 sea bream, 1 John Dory – about 10 oz of each (other white fish can be substituted)
1 onion, finely chopped
2 tomatoes, quartered
½ glass dry white wine
1¾ pints water
1 tablespoon olive oil, for frying
1 clove garlic, crushed and chopped
pinch saffron
sprigs chervil or parsley

- Scale, and carefully fillet the fish, removing all pinbones with tweezers (the mullet is tricky). Reserve the heads and bones, and the livers of the red mullet.
- Sauté the onion in oil till soft, then add the garlic.
- Put in the bones, and as soon as they start to cook, add the white wine, stirring well, and then add the water. Bring to the boil, skim, and turn down to simmering point.
- Add the tomatoes and saffron and cook for 30 minutes.
- Strain the liquid through a sieve.
- Reheat and reduce in volume slightly, by about a quarter, then add the red mullet livers, liquidised with a little fish stock. Keep hot.
- Cut the red mullet fillets in half, the other fish in quarters, so that each person gets a piece of each type of fish. Season them with salt and pepper and put in a saucepan.

- Pour the hot stock over the fish, and stand over a low heat for 5 minutes without letting it boil.
- Serve in soup bowls garnished with either chervil or chopped parsley.
- Serve with the hot, spicy, Provence relish *rouille* served on thin slices of toast (see next recipe).

FRANCE

Rouille

In spite of its similar flavour, this speciality of Provence is not to be confused with *aioli* (garlic-flavoured mayonnaise).

1 clove garlic
1 egg yolk
6 tablespoons extra virgin olive oil
4 oz cooked potato, mashed
pinch paprika
8 thin slices toast

- Crush the garlic with the flat blade of a large knife, and put it in a food processor with the egg yolk, oil and potato. Whiz, thinning with fish stock if it's too thick.
- Serve on thin slices of toast spinkled with paprika with fish soup.

SPAIN

Fisherman's Soup

Around the coast of Spain the fishermen put any fish they have into the pot, the wider the variety, the greater the interest in the flavour, the emphasis being on the smaller fish which do not fetch a premium price at market. Born of thrift, the soup has the advantage of maximum flavour and character.

SERVES 4 TO 6

2 lb assorted fish (including bass, halibut, hake and any shellfish, such as prawns, mussels, clams or small crabs)
3 tablespoons olive oil
2 cloves garlic, peeled and chopped
1 onion, finely chopped
juice 1 lemon (or sour Seville orange)
1 generous glass sherry or white wine
salt and pepper

- Clean and cut up the fish and scrub the mussels.
- Heat the oil in a large casserole dish, and gently fry the garlic and onion for about 10 minutes.
- Add the pieces of fish (not the shellfish), and about 1½ pints water. Season well and cook covered on a low heat for about 15–20 minutes.
- Strain the soup and remove any bones or pieces of skin.
- Put the fish and soup back into the casserole and add the shellfish, the lemon or orange juice and the sherry.
- Cook for another 5 minutes and serve in the cooking dish with a slice of oven-toasted bread in each person's bowl, or serve croutons separately.

THAILAND

Spicy Mussels

This isn't strictly a Thai dish but one inspired by the essentially hot–sour flavours of Thailand: the combination of chillies, ginger and lemon grass. Other Thai seasonings found in such dishes are *galangal* (similar to ginger root), *kaffir* lime leaves (like the pungent leaves of a lemon tree) and the fermented fish sauce, a gamey version of soy sauce called *nam pla* (in Vietnam the same is known as *nuoc mam*).

STARTER FOR 4

2 lb mussels (about 15 per person) scrubbed and bearded
2 cloves garlic, finely chopped
4 shallots, finely chopped
1 glass dry white wine
4 green chillies (deseeded, finely chopped)
1 stem lemon grass, cut into fine strips, 1 inch long (you can use grated peel and juice of ½ lemon)
4 tablespoons extra virgin olive oil
freshly milled black pepper

- In a heavy saucepan, heat the oil and sweat the shallots and garlic gently for a few minutes till soft but not brown.
- Add the chillies, lemon grass and pepper.
- Raise the heat, and add the wine. Cook fiercely until reduced in volume by half.
- Add the mussels, cover with a lid, and cook until the mussels open, no more than a minute or two, and serve immediately.
- Have a dish to put your empty shells in, and a bowl of water to wash your fingers in afterwards.

CHINA

Steamed Sea Bass

Steaming brings out the delicacy of fish, the spring onions and ginger mask the fishy smells, the dressing of hot oil transforms the appearance of the skin of the fish, and the soy sauce gives a savoury finish. The Chinese would then use chopsticks to pick out the seasoned morsels of flaky fish, eating plain rice from their bowls. You need a suitably large steamer, but you can cut the fish in half and place the two halves together on the serving dish.

Kenneth Lo, the Chinese restaurateur and cooking writer, demonstrated this dish to me. You can of course use other fish, or even steaks or fillets, but it is at its most appealing as a whole fish.

SERVES 4 (AS PART OF A CHINESE MEAL)

1 sea bass, approximately 2 lb
1 carrot, peeled, cut into fine julienne matchsticks
6 spring onions, cut lengthwise into fine strips
1 inch ginger root, finely shredded
1 clove garlic, crushed
generous pinch sugar
pinch salt
3 or 4 tablespoons groundnut or sunflower oil
2 tablespoons light soy sauce

- Make 2 or 3 diagonal cuts through the flesh of the fish through to the bone to ensure even cooking.
- Loosely wrap the fish in aluminium foil, smother with the julienne of carrots, spring onions and ginger.
- Place in the steamer, cover and cook for 7–8 minutes on a high heat. Test with a skewer to see if the fish is tender.
- Lay the fish on a serving dish. Sprinkle with salt and sugar.

- Heat the oil in a frying pan with the clove of garlic, and as soon as the garlic browns, remove it, and pour the sizzling oil on the fish slowly and carefully.
- Drizzle with the soy sauce and serve hot with rice.
- Traditionally, each person breaks off a piece of fish with their chopsticks, and dips it in the sauce.

SPAIN

Oven-Baked Fish
Pescado Al Horno

This is a simple dish in which very fresh, bland fish, is heated in a savoury sauce, baked in the oven. The juices of the fish add richness to the sauce. In Mallorca some sultanas are added to the sauce.

SERVES 4

2–3 lb cod, haddock, sea bream or firm-textured white fish
½ green pepper, deseeded, diced
1 medium onion, diced
1 clove garlic, chopped
1 large tomato, skinned, chopped
1 glass dry white wine
1–2 tablespoons olive oil
thyme, oregano, fresh parsley, bay leaf, for seasoning
salt and pepper.

- If the fishmonger hasn't gutted the fish (whole fish are usually used in Spain), cut open the underside of the belly, remove the innards and discard.

- Rinse under a cold tap. Chop off the head and tail (good for a quick fish stock, so do not throw them away yet).
- With a sharp kitchen knife, follow the line of the bone down each side, easing the flesh gently away from the bone. Lay the fish out on its back, two white sides lying uppermost. (The bone can go in your stock with a bit of onion-peeling and thyme, the basis of a tasty fish soup.)
- Fry the onion and green pepper in oil until soft but not coloured, adding the garlic towards the end of the cooking. Then add the wine, tomato and herbs and season to taste. Simmer for 5 minutes to thicken slightly.
- Oil an oven dish, place the fish in it, covered with the sauce.
- Cover with foil loosely and bake in a hot oven, 400°F, 200°C, gas mark 6, for about 20 minutes till tender, checking it's cooked, as size of the fish and temperature are variable.

CHINA

Crabmeat with Asparagus

The wonderful art of Chinese cooking is the speed with which a dish is prepared. It is essentially fast food, until you count in the often intricate work undertaken by way of preparation – though this can be done well in advance. Also of the essence in Chinese cooking is the freshness of the ingredients, ensuring maximum vitamin and nutritional benefits. This dish, basically a stir-fry, depends for its success on the use of a wok.

SERVES 2 (OR 4, WITH OTHER DISHES)

1½ lb asparagus, cut into 1 inch lengths
4 oz fresh, white crabmeat
2 cloves garlic, chopped
2 inches ginger root, trimmed and shredded
2 spring onions, white part only, sliced
2 tablespoons dry sherry
1 teaspoon salt
4 tablespoons corn oil

For the sauce
4 tablespoons clear vegetable stock
1 tablespoon oyster sauce
½ teaspoon potato flour or cornflour

- Blend the ingredients for the sauce together.
- Heat the wok till it starts to smoke, then pour in half the oil.
- Add the asparagus and two-thirds of the ginger, and toss.
- Then add a tablespoon of sherry, and as soon as it sizzles, reduce the heat, and add the sauce mixture.
- Bring to the boil, cover and cook for about 7 minutes.
- Remove from the pan and keep warm.
- Wash, dry and reheat the wok till it smokes. Pour in the rest of the oil, adding the garlic, spring onions and rest of the ginger.

- Stir in the crabmeat and the rest of the sherry.
- Combine with the asparagus and serve with boiled rice.

CANADA

Salt Fish Cakes

Most of the cod caught off Newfoundland is salted, dried and exported (Spain and Portugal have been the main customers for centuries.) Having so much fresh fish, you wouldn't think they have much use for dried salt cod themselves, but tradition lingers on. This is a cod fish cake cooked in the maritime provinces of North America.

SERVES 4

1 lb boneless salt cod, soaked in cold water overnight
1 lb mashed potatoes
1 small onion, finely chopped or minced
2 tablespoons oil, for frying
1 egg, beaten
4 tablespoons dry breadcrumbs
flour (optional)
2–3 tablespoons parsley, finely chopped
salt and pepper

- Drain the cod then cover it with fresh water in a saucepan and heat slowly until almost, but not quite, boiling. Drain and flake.
- Place the fish in a mixing bowl and stir in the mashed potatoes, onion, butter, beaten egg, parsley, and salt and pepper to taste.
- Shape the mixture into 8 cakes, using a little flour only if necessary to help hold them together.
- Coat in breadcrumbs and fry in hot fat or oil, turning to brown both sides.

ZANZIBAR

Tropical Fish Cakes

An unsophisticated combination of filling carbohydrate and beneficial oily fish, rich in polyunsaturated fatty acids and, happily, a favourite with children. If you're using mackerel the ginger cuts into the richness.

SERVES 4 TO 6

1 tin tuna (or salmon or mackerel) drained of oil, and shredded with a fork
1 lb cooked, mashed potato
1 clove garlic, crushed and chopped
piece green ginger, grated
salt, pepper and cayenne (to taste)
1 or 2 eggs, beaten
fat, for shallow frying

- Mix the potato and tuna with the garlic and ginger, season, and pat into cakes 3 inches across and 1 inch thick.
- Dip in beaten egg and shallow fry till brown on each side, about 3 minutes each.

SPAIN

Kidneys with Mushrooms and Sherry

Riñones al Jerez

Offal is free of fat, and as long as you do not use it as part of a hefty mixed grill, which is bad for an overstressed heart, it is economical and nourishing. This particular dish is one that migrated successfully to Paris bistros, where it is cooked with butter, not oil.

SERVES 4

1 lb lambs' kidneys (or you can use other kidneys)
½ lb mushrooms (tiny button mushrooms are best)
2 medium tomatoes, very ripe and juicy
1 clove garlic
1 sherry glass dry sherry or same amount dry white wine
salt and pepper
a little flour
olive oil

- Gently fry the garlic in oil without browning, then add the chopped tomatoes and cook until they have been reduced to a dryish purée and then sieve.
- Skin and quarter the kidneys, removing the core with a sharp knife. Roll them very lightly in a little flour seasoned with salt and pepper (or toss them in a paper bag for ease).
- Wash the button mushrooms. If large, halve or quarter them, but do not use mushrooms with open black gills as they will discolour the sauce.
- Heat the mushrooms in 2 tablespoons olive oil, tossing them about until they begin to sweat their juices. Put a lid over them while you shake them. Remove them with a slotted spoon.
- In the same fat, sauté the kidneys, adding a little more olive oil if necessary.
- Combine the mushrooms and kidneys, turn up the heat and pour in the sherry or white wine, stirring well for a minute.
- Lower the heat, add the tomato sauce, stir, cover the pan and leave to simmer for 3–4 minutes.
- Check the seasoning and add freshly milled black pepper.
- The texture of the dish will depend on the quality of the mushrooms and tomato sauce, but it should not be too dry. If necessary, moisten with a little stock to give plenty of sauce.
- Serve with plain rice.

GREECE

Moussaka

The Greeks have made this dish their own, although it originally comes from Romania. It's deliciously simple and reheats well, too. Make sure the fat is cut off the lamb or else it becomes unpleasantly greasy (and unhealthy too).

SERVES 4

1 lb aubergine
1 medium onion, sliced
1 can tomatoes, chopped
½ lb minced or chopped lamb (free of fat)
½ pint chicken stock

White sauce
½ pint milk
1 oz flour
1 tablespoon olive oil
1 egg
grated cheese
salt and pepper

- Slice the aubergine thinly, leaving the skin on.
- To remove the excess moisture in aubergines, and also the bitter flavour in some older aubergines, sprinkle with salt, stand the slices in a colander with a weighted plate on top, and let them drain for 30 minutes. Then wash free of the salt, and mop dry.
- In a tablespoon or two of olive oil, lightly fry the onion, finely chopped.
- Remove with a slotted spoon and fry the lamb, minced or chopped very fine with a sharp knife.
- Finally, fry the aubergine slices, a few at a time.
- Make a tomato sauce by simmering the chopped tomatoes for 10 minutes, adding a sprig of thyme and seasoning, and strain through a sieve.
- Make a white sauce by heating the oil in a pan, stirring in the flour, and gradually stirring in ½ pint boiling milk until it thickens.
- Off the heat, beat in an egg. Leave the sauce to cool.

- Line the bottom and sides of an oven dish with the aubergine slices.
- Put on top the layer of minced lamb, cover with chicken stock, smother with the fried onions, then add a layer of tomato sauce.
- Finally pour on the white sauce and dust with a little grated cheese.
- Bake in a moderate oven, 350°F, 180°C, gas mark 4, for 30–50 minutes, until the top is golden.

ITALY

Rabbit with Green Olives

The healthiest alternative to traditional meat is game. But rabbit serves the same function. This is a variation on a country dish, given to me by the Italian cookery teacher, Carla Tomasi.

MAIN COURSE FOR 4

1 whole rabbit cut into 4 joints
6 green olives, preserved in oil and water (preferably not brine), chopped small
1 oz stem ginger, grated
1 teaspoon dried oregano
2 tablespoons extra virgin olive oil
salt and pepper

- In a heavy oven dish, brown the rabbit in the oil over a high heat.
- Add the green olives, ginger and seasoning, put the lid on, and transfer to a hot, preheated oven, 400°F, 200°C, gas mark 6, and cook for 30 minutes.
- In Italy this might be served with ½-inch-thick slab of *castagnaccio*, a flat cake made with chestnut flour, cream, pine nuts and raisins.

FRANCE

Light Chicken Liver Pâté

Pâté is no longer a dish to highly recommend, though chicken livers contain nutrients invaluable to a good diet, because traditionally it is combined with a good deal of pork fat. But that is not the case in this recipe, devised by one of the greatest chefs in Provence, Roger Vergé.

SERVES 6

12–15 chicken livers
½ lb white breadcrumbs
½ pint cold milk
3 tablespoons onions, chopped
2 tablespoons olive oil
1 egg yolk
pinch thyme
1 tablespoon parsley, finely chopped
salt, freshly ground pepper

- Trim the livers, cutting away the membranes and greenish parts.
- Soak in 4 tablespoons milk for 2 hours, drain, and discard milk.
- Pat dry with absorbent paper. Season with salt and pepper.
- Heat the oil in a frying pan, and when very hot, fry the livers, turning rapidly with a wooden spatula, till browned.
- Remove them with a slotted spoon, and drain in a colander.
- Lower the heat and fry the onions in the same pan for about 10 minutes, until golden brown.
- Soak the bread in the remainder of the milk and when soft, squeeze between your fingers to remove the surplus liquid.
- Chop the livers finely, then put them in a wide pan with the breadcrumbs, egg yolk, thyme and parsley.
- Stir well on a low heat for 5 minutes, adding a little milk if the mixture dries out.
- Turn out into a buttered terrine dish, pressing down firmly, and cover with oiled or greaseproof paper. Chill for 24 hours.

INDIA

Chicken Tikka Masala

This speciality of the Punjab from the north of India swept the sub-continent, and has now become a favourite flavour in the supermarkets (*tikka* isn't actually a flavour – the word means a 'morsel' or 'tit-bit'). In India this dish is a whole marinated chicken roasted or baked in a tandoori oven. This is a version easily cooked at home, using chicken pieces. Prepare the chicken in the marinade at least 4–6 hours before barbecuing, grilling or roasting.

SERVES 4

1 chicken, quartered (or 4 chicken pieces, legs or breasts as preferred)
½ onion
2 cloves garlic, chopped
1 inch piece ginger, peeled and chopped
1 green chilli, chopped

Spices
1 dessertspoon garam masala (equal quantities of cumin seed, black peppercorns, cinnamon, cloves, cardamom seeds, dry-roasted in a frying pan and ground, with a pinch of nutmeg)

red and yellow food colouring (or 1 dessertspoon paprika powder)
1 large carton plain yoghurt
juice ½ lemon
1 teaspoon salt

- Skin the chicken pieces, cut each in half, and prick all over with a fork.
- Make several slashes with a knife, cutting to the bone, put in a bowl and sprinkle with salt and lemon juice and leave for half an hour.
- Meanwhile, put the yoghurt, onion, garlic and spices into a blender and whiz to a cream. Strain.
- Mop the chicken pieces dry with absorbent paper, and paint with food colour, or rub with paprika.
- Put in a bowl covered with the marinade and leave for 4–6 hours.
- To cook, preheat the grill to very high, or set the oven to its highest, 475°F, 240°C, gas mark 9.
- Shake off the excess marinade, brush the chicken with oil, and grill for 20 minutes on one side, 10 minutes on the other (not too close to the grill), or roast for 25–30 minutes on a grid in the oven, or in a shallow pan. Test with a skewer.
- Take the chicken off the bone.
- Serve with salad and wedges of lemon, with lemon-flavoured or saffron rice.

USA

Cajun Chicken Casserole

Cajun is the indigenous cooking of New Orleans, a corruption of 'Arcadian', the name given to French immigrants to Canada, who immediately headed south to better gastronomic climes. The use of flour as a roux to thicken sauces is the French influence, the spices they picked up from local Indians.

SERVES 6

3 chicken joints
8 oz pinto beans or white beans
bunch fresh herbs – parsley, thyme, sage, bay leaf, (tied together)
1 tablespoon olive oil
1 oz butter
2 tablespoons olive oil
1 onion, finely chopped
1 red pepper, deseeded, sliced
3 heaped tablespoons cajun seasoning
2 heaped tablespoons plain flour
1 vegetable stock cube

- Soak the beans in plenty of cold water overnight, drain, put into a pan, cover with fresh cold water and bring to the boil.
- Add the oil and herbs and simmer for 45 minutes or until the beans are tender. Remove the herbs and drain the beans, reserving the liquid.
- In a large frying pan heat half the olive oil and cook the onions till brown.
- Add the red peppers towards the end of the cooking, to soften but not to brown.
- Skin the chicken joints. Put the cajun spices and flour into a bag and toss the chicken joints in it.
- Add the remaining oil and butter to the frying pan, heat and fry the chicken joints, turning frequently, for about 10 minutes, until browned.
- Put the cooked beans, onion, peppers and chicken into a large casserole dish.
- Bring ½ pint of the bean cooking liquid to the boil and dissolve the vegetable stock cube in it and pour over the beans, cover with a lid and cook in a preheated oven, 350°F, 180°C, gas mark 4, for 45 minutes to 1 hour, when the chicken should be tender.
- Serve with plain rice, and perhaps garlic bread.

HUNGARY
Goulash

Hungary's most famous dish, and also the most misunderstood when transferred to other countries, where it often appears as a thick mixture of meat and tomato sauce. Tomato is the least of the ingredients and its red colour and unique flavour is entirely derived from the flavour of authentic Hungarian paprika which is well worth its premium price in delicatessens and in a different class from paprika from elsewhere. The potatoes not only provide a carbohydrate balance to the protein of the meat, but also absorb the hauntingly delicious flavours of this very soupy stew.

SERVES 4

1 lb stewing beef, trimmed into cubes
4 oz ox hearts, diced
4 oz smoked ham or gammon, or belly of pork, diced
1 large onion, chopped
1 green pepper, deseeded, chopped
1 large tomato, quartered
1 lb potatoes, peeled and cubed
2 cloves garlic
1 tablespoon paprika
¼ teaspoon caraway seeds
salt
2 pints lukewarm water
pork fat or vegetable oil

For the dumplings
3 tablespoons plain flour
1 egg
salt

- Fry the onions gently in the fat until they are transparent but not brown.
- Turn up the heat and add the cubed and diced meat, stirring to sear it.
- Chop the garlic, crush with the caraway seeds in a mortar, blend

with the paprika and stir it into the meat and onions.

- Add the warm water, bring to the boil, cover, and lower the heat. Simmer for 1 hour, then add the peppers and tomato and cook for another half an hour.
- Add the potatoes and cook until they and the meat are tender – another half an hour. Season to taste.
- To make the dumplings, stir the flour and salt into the egg to form a firm dough. Leave for half an hour.
- Shape the dough with a teaspoon to make small balls and add them to the goulash 2–3 minutes before serving. (They are cooked when they rise to the surface.)
- Serve in soup bowls.

ITALY

Harlequin Omelette

This a picnic or party piece, an omelette layered in three colours, as tasty to eat as it is appealing to the eye. The instructions may seem lengthy, but you are doing no more than make three omelettes. This really is a dish to reserve for those occasions when you do have first class ingredients, fresh, free-range eggs and summer-ripe tomatoes – the best for this omelette are Italian. It is better to use drained, canned tomatoes than tasteless unripe, Dutch greenhouse tomatoes.

SERVES 4 TO 6

9 eggs
1 lb ripe tomatoes
1 lb spinach
2 oz Gruyère cheese, grated
8 tablespoons whipping cream
8 tablespoons extra virgin olive oil
2 cloves garlic, peeled but not chopped
pinch thyme
pinch nutmeg
salt and freshly ground pepper

- Skin and deseed the tomatoes (plunge them into boiling water for 40 seconds, then put under cold water to loosen their skins). Chop into rough cubes.
- Heat 2 tablespoons olive oil in a pan till a blue haze rises, and quickly cook the tomatoes with the thyme and a pinch of salt, till the moisture evaporates.
- Drain, chop and set aside, leaving them to cool on a plate.
- Wash the spinach carefully and remove any tough stems. In a large pan heat 3 tablespoons olive oil till blue haze rises, add the spinach, garlic and a pinch of salt. Cook till the moisture evaporates, stirring with a wooden spoon.
- Remove the garlic cloves, and leave the spinach to cool on another plate.
- Break 3 eggs into 3 separate bowls. To the first, add the spinach, 3 tablespoons cream, nutmeg, salt and pepper, and whisk together. To the second, add the tomatoes, 2 tablespoons cream, salt and pepper and whisk. To the third, add the Gruyère, 2 tablespoons cream, salt and pepper and whisk.
- Preheat the oven to 250°F, 120°C, gas mark ½.
- Pour the tomato mixture into a well-oiled terrine and stand it in a bain-marie (or a baking dish half-filled with hot water) and bake for 15 minutes.
- Then gently pour in the Gruyère mixture and bake for another 15 minutes. Pour in the spinach mixture and bake for 15 minutes.
- Let it rest in a warm place for 15 minutes before turning it out. It can be eaten hot, but for a picnic dish, leave it to cool.
- Serve in tricolour slices and dribble with extra virgin olive oil.

TUNISIA

Spicy Scrambled Eggs

In Tunisia harissa paste (see page 252) is used as freely as we use salt and pepper. You'll have to decide how much paste to add, using very little the first time. Then you may find it becomes addictive.

SERVES 4

8 large eggs
1 tablespoon tomato purée
1 teaspoon harissa (home-made or bought)
3 cloves garlic, chopped finely
1 teaspoon ground coriander
1 teaspoon caraway seeds, crushed or ground
½ teaspoon paprika powder
1 teaspoon salt
stoned black olives, for garnish
parsley
olive oil (or vegetable oil) for cooking

- Beat the eggs thoroughly in a bowl.
- Heat about 3 tablespoons oil in a wide, non-stick pan, and fry the garlic on a low heat till it starts to colour but doesn't darken.
- Dilute the tomato paste with four times its volume in water, and add to the pan with the harissa paste, spices and salt, and cook gently for 5 minutes.
- Pour in the eggs, stirring steadily, still on the lowest heat, and cook the eggs till they are set, for 5–10 minutes. The more slowly you cook it the more delicate the texture.
- Serve hot, garnished with olives and parsley, with good bread to make a satisfying but light lunch dish.
- Tunisians like this very hot and add more harissa than the amount given above.

HONG KONG

Stir-Fried Eggs

The Californian-born cook, Ken Hom, has introduced many modern Chinese dishes which have come to the West through Hong Kong. Here East meets West as American sweetcorn replaces the more traditional green pea. You don't have to use a wok, but once you've started using one you'll find dozens of uses for it although stir-frying is its most useful function, especially as you can cook quite large quantities of rice or vegetables with very little oil.

SERVES 4

4 eggs, beaten
1 lb fresh sweetcorn (or 10 oz canned or frozen) or peas
1 dozen spring onions, not too finely chopped
2 inches fresh ginger root, peeled, finely shredded or chopped
salt
groundnut oil (or vegetable oil) for cooking

- Heat a wok or large frying pan till very hot, then add a tablespoon of oil and the spring onions and ginger.
- Let them sizzle fiercely for 10 seconds, then add the sweetcorn (or peas), and, still on a high heat, stir-fry for 2 minutes.
- Turn down the heat to medium and stir in the beaten egg, adding the salt, and cook for a few minutes till set.
- Serve splashed with soy sauce.
- It is a very quick, light lunch, ample when served with good bread.

BULGARIA

Yoghurt

The *Lactus bulgaricus* is the culture which turns milk to yoghurt. If you decide you want to make more of yoghurt in your repertoire of dishes it's a good idea to cut costs by making your own. Although you can buy an electric yoghurt maker, it's easy enough without, since it's a naturally occurring product. Use it in Balkan dishes, or as the Indian summer drink, *lassi*.

MAKES 2 PINTS

2 pints milk *1 teaspoon live yoghurt*

- Using a wide, shallow pan, preferably non-stick, bring the milk to simmering point.
- At the lowest heat possible (not more than 203°F, 95°C) cook for about 15 minutes till reduced by about one-third of its volume.
- Leave the milk to cool till warm enough to put the back of your fingers on to the surface without having to remove them (if you have a thermometer that's 115°F, 46°C).
- Whisk the yoghurt into the milk. Transfer it to a suitable bowl, cover with clingfilm, and put in a warm place, such as an airing cupboard, overnight. (It's a good idea to wrap the bowl in a towel and slip it into a plastic bag to maintain its temperature.)
- The following day it will have set.
- Store in the fridge.

INDIA

Mint and Onion Raita

A *raita* is a cross between a salad and a relish and can incorporate all kinds of vegetables – potato, aubergine, bhindi (okra), carrot – dressed with yoghurt.

SERVES 4

1 onion, chopped small or in thin rings
1 dozen fresh mint leaves, chopped
1 green chilli, deseeded, chopped
4–6 fl oz natural yoghurt
pinch sugar
pinch salt
pinch paprika

- Beat the yoghurt with the salt and sugar and combine with the onion and mint.
- Chill for ½ hour or longer.
- Sprinkle with paprika before serving.

INDIA

Lassi

This delicious cooling summer drink is plain yoghurt, diluted with water, and served plain or sweetened according to taste, with a dusting of freshly roasted, freshly ground cumin seeds. See the previous page for yoghurt.

SERVES 4

8 fl oz yoghurt	*pinch salt (or sugar to taste)*
2 pints water	*1 teaspoon ground cumin*

- Whisk the yoghurt and water vigorously.
- Season with salt or sugar and dust with cumin.

SYRIA

Yoghurt Cheese
Labna

Yoghurt cheese is made like cottage cheese, soured and hung to drain in muslin. It can be served with salads, in pitta bread, or with honey as a dessert. It is easy to make yoghurt at home (see page 223), and is a sensible thing to do if you eat a lot of it.

SERVES 4

1 pint yoghurt	*crushed dried mint, or chopped fresh mint, to taste*
salt and pepper	*olive oil, for sprinkling*
crushed garlic, to taste	

- Line a colander with a thin piece of muslin and pour in the yoghurt. Leave it for several hours for the whey to drain off (the longer you leave it, the firmer the cheese will be).
- Season the drained yoghurt with salt and pepper and mix in the garlic and mint. Sprinkle the olive oil over the top.
- Cover and keep in the refrigerator if you are not going to eat it right away.
- You can also serve the cheese with honey, as a dessert.

6

FRUIT SALADS AND PUDDINGS

Crême Brulée, Bavarois and Black Forest Gâteau have no place in this collection – they can't be squeezed under the narrow apex of the Healthy Eating Pyramid.

In any case, desserts are an area of self-indulgence which people know best how to satisfy without any further encouragement. In many parts of the Orient dessert is fruit, and only fruit. Given the wonderful choice of fresh exotic fruit in the tropics that is no hardship.

The traditional British way with a pudding, and this was before central heating, was a suet pudding, an indigestible mixture of flour and fat occasionally elevated to moments of greatness, as in a lemon-scented, buttery, syrupy Sussex Pond Pudding. We're always being lulled into believing that cream is a deliciously wicked excess (to allow ourselves as often as possible). There's no denying that while the rich, mature flavour of Devon and Cornish clotted cream takes some beating (and there's room under the Pyramid for an occasional indulgence) the use of double cream as a matter of course is an area of concern. On the other hand there's merit in some of the solid nursery favourites of the British childhood and a few have been included here, partly for nostalgic reasons. Alas, they will not taste as they did in our childhood, because we've traded convenient, factory bread which doesn't stale for the full-flavoured bread of our childhood, which did dry out and stale and therefore mopped up the milk or fruit juices.

Rich, egg-based puddings, along with cream don't really fit under the Pyramid except in the area of soufflés, where a little egg goes an extremely long way.

Guide to exotic fruits

Babaco Pale, yellowy-green, ribbed fruit the size of a medium marrow, entirely edible, the texture of a water melon, tasting of very dilute, unsweetened lemon juice. It gives a certain texture, sliced into a fruit salad, and is mildy refreshing. In the Brazilian jungle it will ripen to deep purple and hangs from the trees in clusters, like bats. Ours are grown under glass in Guernsey. A novelty.

Carambola Ribbed green fruit, which slices thinly into lovely star shapes. Tastes of verjuice, the juice of unripe grapes. Poach the slices in sugar syrup for 2 or 3 minutes before using in a fruit salad.

Granadilla Four times larger than a passion fruit, with a dessertspoonful of meltingly beautiful seeds the size of salmon caviar. Very romantic but lacking true passion.

Guava Beautifully scented, pippy, South American jungle fruit, which is lovely when lightly poached with sugar. Put it into your fruit bowl and you'll know by the perfume when it is ready to use.

Kiwi fruit Now much maligned by diners-out, who welcomed its decorative debut in *nouvelle cuisine* in the 1970s. A perfect modern commercial package with the firm feel of a new tennis ball. It was known as the Chinese gooseberry until the New Zealanders hijacked it. In fact the new-generation kiwis are being grown in France and Italy, and have less of the sharp, gooseberry character of the antipodean variety, which you may or may not prefer. It slices prettily into fruit salads.

Kumquat This is the most delightful little member of the citrus family. Eaten whole, it fills the mouth with the bitter-sweet sensation of the peel, before exploding into acidity. Slice it into a fruit salad.

Lychee An object of extraordinary loveliness, with its scaly, dragon-coloured skin, moonstone-coloured, slippery, sweet flesh, and an ebony stone, like a shiny sculpture. Even canning cannot destroy its sensual beauty. It makes a lovely sorbet. The *rambutan* is a lychee dressed in a fright-wig.

Mango The taste of mango in a plain fruit salad gives it a masterly exotic touch. The smaller, Indian, *alphonso* mango is giving way to the larger, Brazilian, *haden* mango, preferred here because of its ripe, maroon blush. It is perfect for the modern supermarket world as it ripens slowly and patiently once picked, though you may need to keep one in a warm kitchen for weeks rather than days to appreciate its full richness. Cut off its 'cheeks', turn the skin inside-out and cut a criss-cross pattern deep into the flesh to get neat cubes for use in salads.

Passion fruit The ultimate in perfume and keen flavour. The more wrinkled these brown ping-pong balls are, the greater the intensity of the essence inside, which represents no more than a teaspoon of slippery, yellow pips in a cerise jacket. Perfume a fruit salad with a few spoonfuls. Press the juice through a sieve to flavour the sweet sauces of soufflés. Boil the skins to extract their flavour, too, but never bring the actual juice to the boil. The passion is spiritual, not lustful, for the markings of its beautiful flower were used by Catholic priests in Latin America to illustrate the sufferings of Christ on the cross.

Pawpaw (Papaya) A tender and lovely fruit with the melting texture of avocado, the colour of poached salmon, bursting with seeds which could pass for metal-coloured grains of beluga caviar (strangely, they taste of watercress). Unfortunately, the pawpaw doesn't like our climate and is hard to nurse out of a soapy, bitter sulk. Persevere, put it in a brown paper bag in the kitchen with an apple or potato, which is an old wives' remedy for ripening any sort of fruit. Eat with a splash of lemon juice. It contains *papain*, a protein-eating enzyme, and you can layer meat with the skins to tenderise it.

Physalis (Cape gooseberry) Orange-coloured berry, the size of a cherry tomato, now sold in see-through boxes, stripped of its pretty, papery brown petals (those with red petals are called Chinese lanterns). The skin is bitter, which may explain why it has been used as *petits fours*, the berry dipped in sweet, icing-sugar fondant, giving a bitter-sweet sensation.

Pineapple The most decorative of all fruits, even incorporated into architectural designs, and worthy of its place in the fruit bowl for this reason alone. Pineapple juice contains a ferociously strong enzyme that eats protein. Workers in canning factories wear protective gloves to stop their skin from being eaten away. The juice is a great tenderiser for pork and chicken; use it in marinades. Don't use it in jellies, as it dissolves gelatine, which is a protein.

Pitahaya One of the marvellous new surprises on the shelves. It is an utterly superior cousin of the prickly pear, with a soft, sweet, marshmallow pith inside, dotted with innumerable black (edible) seeds. The pitahaya is adored by children.

Sharon fruit The Israelis developed this ready-to-eat version of the persimmon, a fruit so puckeringly tannic when unripe you would never eat a second one. The sharon fruit has had the astringency bred out of it, and now you can eat it ripe or unripe without ill-effects. It looks like a tomato, cuts like a custard jelly, has no seeds, and it ought to be a winner. It's all right, but somehow it tastes like a fruit put together by a committee.

GUADELOUPE

Exotic Fruit Salad

Salade des Fruits Exotiques

The fruit might come from Guadeloupe, but the inspiration for the syrup is that of a Parisian chef, Alain Senderens. His spiced syrup pulls all the flavours together. The fruit salad needs to be chilled for at least 2 hours. Tropical fruit, especially mango, pineapple, kiwi fruit and passion fruit, give a tremendous life to a fruit salad of, say, cubes of melon, apple or pear, seeded grapes, skinned segments of orange, lemon or grapefruit.

SERVES 4

For the syrup
3 oz sugar
1 pint water
zest of lime, orange and a lemon
1 inch peeled green ginger, grated
pinch of star anise
5 coriander seeds
1 clove

mango
pineapple
kiwi fruit
passion fruit
melon
apple
pear
grapes
orange
lemon
grapefruit

- Bring the ingredients for the syrup to the boil, turn off the heat and leave to stand. When cool, strain the syrup over the prepared fruit of your choice and store in the fridge until needed.

WEST INDIES

Christophene Fruit Salad

The pale, green christophene is one of the more unfamiliar fruits on the Caribbean stall. They are crisp and juicy and add an unusual, appley character to a fruit salad.

SERVES 4 (IN A FRUIT SALAD)

2 or 3 christophenes
2–3 oranges, peeled and segmented or cubed
2 grapefruit, peeled (same as oranges)
2 mangoes, peeled, cubed
8 oz pineapple squares
exotic syrup (see page 231)

- Christophenes leave a sticky residue like glue when you peel them. To prevent this, wipe a teaspoon of vegetable oil on your hands with a paper towel before you start.
- Peel the fruit, halve it and remove the stone-like core.
- Use a potato peeler or kitchen knife to shave it into thin slices.
- Chill in a bowl of water, acidulated with a squeeze of lemon juice, overnight.
- Use as apples (or serve with a mayonnaise of avocado or hummus dip).
- For the fruit salad, combine all the fruits with a few spoonfuls of exotic syrup, and chill for several hours before serving.

LEBANON

Dried Apricot and Prune Salad

Although this fruit salad is particularly satisfying in winter when summer fruits are not around, it is good at any time and keeps well in the fridge. In fact, it needs to be made two days in advance. Prunes used in this way give a rich, deep and sensuous flavour. Vary the ingredients, using canned or dried figs, adding walnuts or flaked almonds as a garnish, blending in some freshly segmented oranges, or chopped apple at the moment of serving, or, for a more authentic touch, sprinkling with separated pomegranate seeds.

SERVES 4

1 lb prunes
½ lb dried apricots
2 oz sugar
1 oz fresh ginger (or preserved ginger, if fresh is unavailable)

- Make at least 2 days ahead.
- Soak the prunes and apricots separately in cold water, for about 12 hours or overnight.
- When they are soft, put them in a saucepan with the sugar and prune water, strained if necessary.
- Peel and slice the ginger and put it in with the fruits, bring to the boil and simmer until the fruit is tender – about 1 hour.
- Allow to cool, and transfer to a bowl.
- Steep for at least a day, before serving.

LATVIA

Cranberry Kisel

This 'jellied' dessert is typical of northern Europe, the cornflour blending with the juices to produce a clear, shining liquid, which is allowed to cool and set. It's a technique common with fruits collected from the wild in field and forest, such as Swedish longanberries, whortleberries, bilberries and blueberries.

SERVES 4

½ lb cranberries
2 teaspoons cornflour
6 oz sugar (or to taste)
1 stick cinnamon

- Pick over the berries, wash them quickly without soaking and put them in a pan with 2 fl oz water.
- Simmer until the skins burst, then rub them through a sieve.
- Dissolve 5 oz sugar in 2 fl oz water and add the cranberry pulp and juice with the cinnamon.
- Simmer for 10 minutes, then remove the cinnamon.
- Blend the cornflour with 1 tablespoon cold water and stir in the cranberries.
- As soon as the juices thicken, remove the pan from the heat and pour the kisel into a serving bowl.
- When the dessert cools, a crust will form on the top. Sprinkle the remaining 1 oz sugar over this.
- Chill and serve cold with fromage frais, thick yoghurt or rosettes of whipped cream.

ENGLAND

Mother's Bread Pudding

Before the sliced, factory-made loaves were invented in the 1960s white bread used to go stale in a day or two. My grandmother used to make beautiful puddings with day-old bread: Summer Pudding oozing the juice of summer berries; Apple Charlotte, thin slices of white bread, fried in clarified butter, lining a basin, filled with spiced apple purée and baked for 20 minutes; Poor Knights of Windsor, rounds of bread dipped in beaten egg yolk, fried in clarified butter and sprinkled with sugar. But this is my mother's recipe.

SERVES **4**

¾ pint milk	*1 egg, beaten*
4 oz breadcrumbs	*2 oz sultanas or currants*
1 tablespoon brown sugar	*1 teaspoon mixed spice*
1 oz butter	*pinch salt*

- In a bowl mix the breadcrumbs and sugar.
- Heat the milk with the butter until it melts, and pour over the breadcrumbs, adding the mixed fruit, spice, beaten egg and pinch of salt.
- Bake in a preheated, low oven, 325°F, 170°C, gas mark 3, for 45 minutes.

ENGLAND

Granny's Bread and Butter Pudding

The celebrated Swiss chef, Anton Mosimann, of television fame, has made his re-invention of English bread and butter pudding into a signature dish, though we traditionalists would consider his version is really French, consisting of delicately baked slices of brioche in a classic chef's custard. This is my grandmother's recipe. But the original goes back to Tudor times.

SERVES 4

6 slices white bread
butter, for thinly spreading
apricot jam
½ pint semi-skimmed (or whole) milk
2 whole eggs and 1 yolk
1 tablespoon sultanas (or traditionally, sugar)

- Make 3 sandwiches, spread with the apricot jam. Cut off the crusts (give them to the birds). Cut the sandwiches into squares and put them in an oven dish.
- Beat the milk, eggs (sugar if using) and pour over the sandwich squares (adding the sultanas).
- Leave to soak for at least 30 minutes.
- Place the oven dish in a larger tin, half-filled with hot water (as a bain marie) and bake in a moderate oven, preheated to 350°F, 180°C, gas mark 4, and cook until puffy and golden.

ENGLAND

Summer Pudding

A superb seasonal delight, bringing together the early summer's soft fruit, running with thick, tart, crimson or purple juices. According to availability, use raspberries, redcurrants, blackcurrants, whitecurrants, strawberries, (quartered).

SERVES 4 TO 6

about 12 thin slices yesterday's bread
¾ lb raspberries
¾ lb redcurrants
caster sugar

- Wash and drain the fruit. Remove the stalks from the raspberries. With a fork, pull the redcurrants from their stalks.
- Put the fruit in a saucepan with enough sugar to slightly sweeten, cover and heat gently until the juices run, but don't allow it to cook. Strain off a few tablespoons of the juice and reserve.
- Cut the crusts off the bread. Butter a 2 pint pudding basin or soufflé dish and line the bottom and sides with the bread slices, trimming each piece to make a neat fit. Keep some pieces to make a lid.
- Pile the fruit into the basin and cover with bread.
- Cover the pudding with a plate and put a heavy weight on top, then chill in the fridge for 8 hours or so, long enough for the juice to penetrate and soak the bread with its rich flavour.
- To serve, put a large plate over the basin, turn upside-down and ease the pudding out gently. There may be some bald patches where the juice hasn't soaked in, so pretty it up with the juices you have reserved.
- Serve alone or with crême fraiche, fromage frais, Greek yoghurt or cream.

ENGLAND

Rice Pudding

An incredibly small amount of rice is needed to make this satisfying dish. You need Carolina rice, a glutinous, absorbent rice suitable only for puddings and desserts. For Sunday best, add whole milk, or as a high day luxury, whole milk with added cream. It's gilding the lily, really, but you can add a handful of sultanas to enrich it even more.

SERVES 4

2 oz Carolina (pudding) rice
2 pints semi-skimmed (or whole) milk
3 teaspoons sugar
piece of zest of lemon (or a bay leaf)
grated nutmeg

- Mix the ingredients in an oven dish, grating the nutmeg on top.
- Bake in a low oven, 300°F, 150°C, gas mark 2.
- After 1 hour, remove the pudding and stir. Put it back in the oven for about another hour, until it's firm and has a nice blistering skin.
- An alternative, sweeter, flavouring to lemon peel is a teaspoon of cinnamon powder.

SYRIA

Sweet Semolina
Mamonnia

In the United Kingdom we would serve this as a pudding, but sweetened semolina is the breakfast porridge of Syria, and varies in thickness of texture and sweetness according to taste. Those with memories of school semolina, probably made with water and not milk, should give it another chance. It's delicious.

SERVES 4

6 oz semolina
1 pint milk and water, half-and-half
2 oz butter (or a little more)
4 oz sugar
cinnamon
almonds, chopped

- Gently fry the semolina in the butter in a large saucepan for 5 minutes over a low heat, stirring with a wooden spoon.
- Pour the milk and water into another saucepan, add the sugar and bring to the boil, stirring until the sugar has dissolved.
- Add the liquid to the semolina, stirring all the time.
- Continue to stir over a low heat until the mixture has thickened to a cream.
- Remove from the heat and leave to stand for 15 minutes.
- Serve in small bowls, sprinkled with a little cinnamon and, if you like, chopped almonds.

SWITZERLAND

Passion Fruit Soufflé

The soufflé is a weapon in the armoury of the French classical cook and is usually very rich. The Swiss chef, Fredy Girardet, adopted the passion fruit to provide a sensational level of flavour in a soufflé which is the essence of lightness. It is very easy to make. A luxury which doesn't break the bounds of sensible eating.

SERVES 4

½ pint passion fruit juice (16, or so, passion fruit)
2 egg yolks
4 egg whites
5 oz caster sugar
unsalted butter

- Halve the passion fruit, remove the pulp, squeeze it through a sieve with the back of a spoon and reserve.
- Beat the egg yolks with half the sugar till fluffy.
- Whisk the egg whites to a snow, add the remaining sugar and continue beating, till stiff.
- Add 4 tablespoons of passion fruit juice to the yolk mixture, and stir in one-third of the whites firmly. Then gently fold in the remainder of the whites.
- Pour into a buttered soufflé mould, or small individual ones.
- Bake in very hot, preheated oven at 430°F, 220°C, gas mark 7, for 12–15 minutes.
- While it cooks, warm the rest of the passion fruit juice in a bain-marie (or small saucepan in a larger pan of boiling water), and serve as a sauce.

ITALY

Zabaglione

A soufflé without all the bother of using the oven, a succulent dessert which makes a small amount of egg go a very long way. It requires a certain *tour de main* or at least some committed and vigorous whisking. Serve hot and frothing in shallow glasses or goblets with sponge fingers.

PER PERSON

1 egg yolk, plus 1 extra for every 3 yolks
1 teaspoon sugar
1 measure marsala wine
pinch salt

- Place all the ingredients in a clean basin and whip together.
- Place the basin over hot (*not boiling*) water, and continue to whisk steadily until stiff. Remove from the water, continue to whisk, then pour into glasses.
- The secret of a successful zabaglione is that it must be brought to boiling point but must not boil or it will curdle.

7

RELISHES

Living at the bottom of the Healthy Eating Pyramid would be pretty dull without seasoning – potatoes without salt, pasta without sauces, rice without spices, beans without chilli.

We British love our relishes and spicy sauces, traditionally, anchovy relish, patum peperium paste (made with anchovies and pepper), mushroom ketchup, Lea and Perrins Worcestershire Sauce, Daddies Sauce, OK Sauce, HP Sauce. Few read the ingredients, or they might be surprised to see that many contain Indian and oriental ingredients – tamarind pulp (a sour fruit), soy sauce, chillies, ginger.

Now we can buy these ingredients fresh, for example green ginger and green chillies. And we have a choice of soy sauces, and strange Vietnamese fermented fish sauces like *nam pla*, Chinese oyster sauce, flavoured oils, roast sesame oil with chilli, and so on.

These are some of the relishes and spice mixtures used in different parts of the world to bring zest and life into their foods. They are easy to make at home and most can be stored in air-tight spice jars, or in the fridge.

The curry powders you buy soon go stale, though many people keep them on their kitchen shelves for years. The seed is roasted to release its aromatic oil, but once it's ground, the oils go rancid, producing a bitter taste. Throw out stale, old, dried spices, and herbs too.

MEXICO

Salsa Cruda

Salsa cruda and *salsa verde* (made with green tomato of the country, *tomatillo*) is served with almost every meal in Mexico and enjoyed much as we use condiments. It is eaten with meat, chicken and egg dishes. You can make it as hot as you dare. In Mexico there are many kinds of chilli peppers and as a general rule they get hotter as they get smaller. Degrees of hotness vary in a single batch. The most prized hot chilli in Britain is the bonnet pepper, small and round, red, yellow and green, a skinny minuscule version of a green bell pepper.

MAKES ABOUT ½ PINT

½ lb tomatoes, skinned and chopped
½ medium onion, chopped
10 sprigs fresh coriander, chopped
4 chilli peppers, deseeded and chopped
Sea-salt to taste
4 tablespoons water

- Combine all the ingredients in a bowl, and serve at the table as a relish, with meat, chicken or egg dishes.

For *salsa verde*

- Blend 1 tin tomatillos, 4 green chillies, 1 chopped onion, 2 crushed cloves garlic, 6 stems green coriander, pinch salt and up to ¼ pint chicken stock or water for 30 seconds in a liquidiser.
- Chill and serve with barbecued meat.

For hot *salsa verde*

- Simmer the above mixture in a pan with 2 tablespoons vegetable oil and extra ¼ pint liquid for 15–30 minutes, until thick.

COLOMBIA

Hot Chilli Relish
Salsa de Aji

This freshly made table relish is automatically put on the table at most meals in Colombia. It is extremely hot. Halve the quantity of chillies if you're not ready for the real thing. Serve with meat, fish and egg dishes.

SERVES 4

1 medium onion, finely chopped
6 oz fresh green chillies, deseeded and finely chopped
1 teaspoon sea-salt

- Combine all the ingredients and purée in a blender.

INDIA

Fresh Mango Relish

A relish made from uncooked fresh fruit is juicier and more piquant than the syrupy chutneys which you buy in jars. Not only are they better for you but they act as a spur to the appetite.

SERVES 4

1 large mango
juice ½ lime (or lemon)
sea-salt
cayenne or chilli pepper

- Slice the mango lengthwise, and cut away the stone. To remove the flesh, use the sharp point of a kitchen knife to make 3 deep cuts, criss-cross, through the flesh, but not through the skin. Turn the skin inside out, and the flesh can be removed in cubes.
- Chop the mango flesh and combine with the lime juice, salt and cayenne pepper.

INDIA

Mango Chutney

An essential relish with curries and rice. It is very easy to make your own, especially when mangoes are cheap.

MAKES A LARGE JAR

1 lb ripe mangoes, peeled
1 oz currants
juice of 1 lime (or lemon)
1 green chilli, deseeded
1 tablespoon oil
1 onion, chopped finely
6 tablespoons red vinegar
3 oz sugar
1 teaspoon mustard seeds
1 teaspoon coriander seeds
2 pieces preserved stem ginger, chopped
large pinch cinnamon
1 teaspoon sea-salt

- Cut the mangoes into ½ inch squares and mix with the currants and lemon juice.
- Fry the onion in the oil till soft, add the chilli and cook for a few minutes.
- Stir in the mangoes and the remainder of the ingredients.
- Cook for 15 minutes.
- Discard the chilli, cool and put in kitchen jar.
- Keep it for at least a week before using, but it improves with keeping longer.

KOREA

Pickled Cabbage
Kim Chee

Like East European Sauerkraut in principle, but not in flavour, *kim chee* is served extremely cold, and the flavour is intensely, tongue-numbingly hot. It is eaten with nearly every meal in Korea. You can get a taste of it at one of the several dozen Korean restaurants in London (a spicy cuisine, much enjoyed by the Japanese who fill the restaurants, and cheaper than Japanese food). The Koreans make this in large quantities and store it in huge earthenware jars buried in the earth under the floors of their houses.

MAKES SEVERAL JARS

2 lb Chinese cabbage (pak choi)
2 tablespoons salt
2 oz cayenne or chilli pepper
2 cloves garlic, crushed and chopped
8 spring onions, whites only, chopped
2 teaspoons sugar

- Cut the cabbage into 1 inch squares, mix with the salt in a large bowl and stand for an hour.
- Rinse it in cold water, and drain well in a colander.
- Mix the remaining ingredients together in a bowl, put a weighted flat board on top and leave to cure for 4 days in a cool place, outdoors preferably, as the smell is quite strong.
- Transfer to glass jars and keep in the fridge.
- Serve cold in small portions, as part of a spicy meal, with rice or noodles.

ITALY

Pesto

Often a plate of pasta needs little more than a relish like this one, *pesto*. *Pesto* means, 'pounded', and it is a paste of pounded herbs and nuts with cheese. Usually it's made with basil, pine nuts and pecorino cheese. But you can make it with parsley or leaf coriander, or with walnuts or almonds or hazelnuts, and with other kinds of grated cheese, such as Parmesan. (If using walnuts, chop separately, and add them untoasted and last, as they are very oily.)

SERVES 4 (OR MORE)

2 bunches basil leaves
2 cloves garlic, peeled and chopped
2 tablespoons pine nuts, toasted
4 oz grated pecorino (or Parmesan) cheese
extra virgin olive oil (up to 4 tablespoons)
½ teaspoon salt

- In a food processor, whiz the garlic and the nuts until finely chopped and gritty, but not a paste.
- Chop the basil by hand finely, and in a bowl mix with the nuts, Parmesan cheese and salt.
- Stir in the oil last, adding enough to make a smooth mixture. All the ingredients should be identifiable, as the pesto should not resemble mayonnaise.
- Serve, unheated, on plain boiled pasta, diluting it with a spoonful or two of the pasta cooking liquid.

INDIA

Curry Spices

You can buy curry powders in tins, but Indians don't. They make their own mixtures known as *masalas*, 'roasting' whole spices in a flat iron pan to release the volatile aromas, then freshly grinding them. Every cook has his or her own mixture, varying the proportions according to taste, or the feeling of the dish. It usually contains chilli, but a *garam masala* does not.

Hot, pungent and strong-flavoured spices such as chilli, ginger powder, mustard seed and turmeric need to be cooked in oil for a few minutes to temper them before continuing the cooking. If they're added to a dish untempered the raw, crude flavour will never cook out, and Indians call the flavour of the final dish 'sharp', a term indicating failure.

Garam masala, a spice mixture from north India, however, contains no sharp ingredients, only 'warm' spices. *Garam* means 'warm'. They are specifically cumin and coriander seeds, cloves and cinnamon. The mixture is often added towards the end of the cooking as it does not need to be tempered. Overleaf are two mixtures you can make up before experimenting with your own mixture. Coriander is mild and lemony in flavour, and is usually in a ratio of two parts coriander to one of cumin, which is strong and spicy.

It's no great hardship to pound spices with a pestle and mortar, although you can speed up the process by using a coffee grinder specially kept for the purpose (or simply wiped clean). Some people buy commercial mixes and keep them for years, unaware of the delights they are missing. Make small amounts frequently, as the flavour, contained in the seeds' natural oil goes rancid and stale once they have been heated and ground.

INDIA

Curry Powder

MAKES 1 SMALL JAR

1 oz coriander seeds
½ teaspoon mustard seeds
½ teaspoon black peppercorns
½ teaspoon fenugreek seeds
4 small dried red chillies
½ teaspoon ground turmeric
½ teaspoon ground ginger

- In a dry pan gently heat the coriander seeds, mustard seeds, peppercorns, fenugreek and chillies until they start to give off an appetising aroma.
- When cool, grind them in a coffee grinder or in a mortar with a pestle. Add the turmeric and ginger powder, and put the mixture in a small jar.

INDIA

Garam Masala

MAKES 1 SMALL JAR

2 teaspoons cumin seeds
4 teaspoons coriander seeds
1 teaspoon cinnamon
1 teaspoon cardamom seeds (dehusked)
½ teaspoon ground black peppercorns
½ teaspoon ground cloves

- In a dry pan heat the cumin, coriander and cardamom seeds till they give off a pungent aroma. Grind them and keep the mixture in a jar.

THAILAND

Curry Paste

If you aren't in a position to buy the exciting curry pastes sold in the few speciality shops which specialise in Thai ingredients, you can make the paste yourself and keep it in a jar, making sure there is a surface film of oil to protect it. Use small amounts in soups, meat, fish and rice dishes.

MAKES 1 SMALL JAR

2 red peppers, deseeded, roughly chopped
1 green pepper, deseeded, chopped
4 oz fresh ginger root, peeled and chopped
3 whole heads garlic, peeled (about 3 dozen cloves)
1 glass dry white wine, or white wine vinegar

Spices
2 teaspoons turmeric
2 teaspoons cardamom seeds, ground
2 teaspoons cinnamon powder
2 teaspoons cumin powder
2 teaspoons ginger powder
2 teaspoons cayenne pepper
1 teaspoon ground fenugreek
groundnut oil or sunflower oil

- Whiz the peppers, garlic, ginger and wine (or vinegar) in a blender, till pulped. In a bowl mix in the spices, and stir in enough oil to make a wet paste.
- Spread on to an oven proof dish and bake in a moderate oven, preheated to 350°F, 180°C, gas mark 4, for ½ hour.
- Using a sieve, drain out the excess oil.
- Scoop the paste into a jar, cover with a thin film of fresh oil and store in the fridge (or freezer).
- Heat the paste in a pan, before adding other ingredients to be cooked in a curry.

MOROCCO

Harissa

This is the essential flavouring which lifts a cous cous on to another plane. Although you can buy it in tins and tubes in some speciality shops, it has a crude flavour compared with the *harissa* you make at home. It is so simple, you can quickly make a supply for a few months in your blender. If you have whole spices, heat them in a frying pan (without fat) until they start to give off their aromas. Grind in a coffee grinder or pound in a mortar.

MAKES 1 SMALL JAR

1 oz dried red chillies
1 clove garlic
1 teaspoon caraway seeds
½ teaspoon ground coriander
½ teaspoon ground cumin
½ teaspoon salt
2 or 3 tablespoons olive oil

- Put the chillies in a teacup, cover with boiling water and leave to soak for 1 hour.
- Drain and chop finely.
- Put them in a blender with the oil, salt and spices, and whiz to a pulp. Put the mixture in a small jar covered with oil, and store in the fridge.
- This quantity will keep in the fridge for a couple of months at least, as long as you keep the surface covered with a little oil.
- Use it sparingly instead of hot sauce or tabasco (dilute with a little hot stock or water).
- The essential accompaniment to cous cous.

YEMEN

Zhug

The hotter the country, the hotter the spices you find they use. This is served at a meal in a saucer as we might use salt and pepper. To make a less fiery relish, which they call *hilbeh*, blend 1 teaspoon zhug with 2 large tomatoes, skinned and deseeded, together with 2 tablespoons fenugreek seeds, ground into powder.

SERVES 4

4 small chilli peppers
1 whole head garlic, peeled
large bunch fresh coriander leaves
4 cardamom pods
1 tablespoon caraway seeds
salt and pepper

- Process all the ingredients together in a blender. Store in a lidded jar.

JAPAN

Gomasio

This is the table spice of Japan, a mixture of coarse salt and toasted sesame seeds, and freely sprinkled on plain rice and vegetables. *Goma* means 'sesame seed'

1 oz coarse sea-salt
2 oz black sesame seeds (or the hulled white seeds)

- In a dry frying pan, lightly toast the seeds until they give off a nutty aroma.
- Pound in a mortar with the sea-salt and store in a small, air-tight jar.

SPAIN

Picada

Picada is a Catalan version of the Italian pesto, a mixture of hazelnuts (or pine nuts, or almonds) blended with garlic, chopped parsley and fried bread, which is stirred into a soup or stew just before serving, to both flavour and thicken it. Almonds can be skinned if first put to soak in a cup of boiling water for 5 minutes.

TO MAKE ABOUT 4 OZ

1 thick slice country bread
1 dozen hazelnuts, dry-fried, skins rubbed off, pounded
1 dozen almonds, skinned
1 tablespoon parsley, finely chopped
2 cloves garlic, crushed and chopped
generous pinch salt
1 or 2 tablespoons olive oil

- In very hot olive oil, fry the bread, crusts removed, on each side till crisp, then allow to cool.
- In a blender (or pestle and mortar) mix the nuts, fried bread, garlic and salt to a paste.
- Stir in the parsley and enough oil to make the paste smooth.

8

GUIDE TO OILS

It is only in the latter part of this century that vegetable oils have become the prime cooking fat the world over. The big exception to this has been the Mediterranean, where the oil of the olive has been used throughout recorded history. Each country used whatever fat was the most easily available: butter in the north of France, goose and duck fat in the south-west of France, beef dripping in Britain and pork fat very widely, especially in China and the Orient. The flavours imparted by these fats, such as *spec* the cured back fat of Hungary, and *pancetta*, the cured fatty bacon of Italy, give a characteristic feel to national dishes.

Fat gives meat its flavour, especially best beef. Pork sausages would be inedible without their pork fat content and French cooking would be miserable indeed without the succulent flavour of butter. But present nutritional wisdom suggests that Western man consumes too much fat, and of the wrong sort. Conforming to these guidelines doesn't mean depriving yourself of these good flavours which contribute to the world's finest dishes, but you can be wise and watchful.

Most of us know now that we should reduce the amount of saturated fat in our diet by reducing our consumption of animal and dairy fats, butter, cream, cheese and egg yolks, and we believe it's okay to let go with unsaturated oils, olive and sunflower oil in particular. This is true only as far as it goes. The government actually recommends as a goal for the year 2,000 that we should bring down all fat and oil consumption until it represents, at most, 30% of our energy intake, but preferably nearer to 15%. They argue that even though unsaturated oils and spreads do not increase blood cholesterol concentration, fat intake may promote obesity and contribute to hypertension.

Beef dripping, lamb fat and lard actually have slightly fewer calories than olive oil. Lard has 4,600 calories to the pound, compared with olive oil, which has 4,650 calories, so eating food with lashings of 'healthy' olive oil will not reduce the threat of obesity. You only have to look at some of the huge matrons of West Africa, Brazil, Greece and India to see the results of high intakes of fat and oil (peanut oil, palm oil, olive oil and ghee, respectively).

I don't believe we should deny ourselves the good flavour of butter, cured pork, beef dripping, but it's sound advice to use them only in order to impart flavour, as a seasoning. For this reason, the great dishes of Belgian *haute cuisine*, such as *waterzoi* (chicken or shellfish poached and served in a bath of butter) or mussels served with bowls of mayonnaise and chips, aren't appropriate to this collection of recipes.

Usually it's not the home cook who errs in the use of fat; it's the innocent shopper, unaware of the hidden fat in many manufactured foods. You need a pocket calculator to assess fat content from the window of nutritional information on not only fatty foods, such as sausages (fried sausages are 1,530 calories to the pound) and hamburgers, chips and crisps, but also unlikely foods, such as pies, biscuits, ice-cream and chocolate. The fat percentage of milk chocolate is high, giving a calorie count of 2,940 per pound. Cheese is another fat whose calorie count is less obvious – cream cheese is 86% fat, a staggering 4,065 calories to the pound (steady on the cheesecake), but Dutch Edam is a modest, by comparison, 1,565 calories to the pound. Stilton and Parmesan are high, 2,385 and 2,100 calories per pound, respectively, but, by way of compensation, are usually eaten in minuscule amounts.

The most useful oils in the kitchen are sunflower, corn, soya bean, cottonseed and groundnut, as they are high in polyunsaturates which have the effect of lowering blood cholesterol. Saturated fats (dripping, butter, lard, and some oils such as palm and coconut) have the opposite effect. In this respect, olive oil is neutral, being mono-unsaturated. It is probably best not to be obsessive about all this, and pick from a range of all the oils to suit taste requirements.

Oil for frying should be heated to 320°F, 165°C, minimum to ensure that what you are frying seals quickly and doesn't become a sponge for the oil. It should not be allowed to rise above 375°F, 190°C, as it starts to disintegrate. If it is smoking, it is too hot. Oil smokes at around 450°F, 230°C, and it goes up in flames at 650°F, 325°C. Olive oil is more combustible, smoking and reaching flash point at a lower temperature.

Olive oil The most delicious table oil, its fruity flavour being ideal for salads. Given its price, it is wasted in frying.

Extra-virgin olive oil A premium oil, and the most expensive cold-pressed, estate-bottled oils, especially those from Lucca in Tuscany, cost four times more than regular oil. Extra virgin olive oils, from Greece and Spain are good value. They are imported by both Provençal and Tuscan oil producers to balance their blends. For a dressing, olive oil is often quite heavy, and can be thinned with tasteless groundnut oil or sunflower oil. It is a source of linoleic acid and other polyunsaturates. Olive oil contains 74% mono-unsaturates.

Sunflower oil The success story of the last decade. It is an oil that has been used in Russia and the Balkans for many years. It is high on the list of healthy oils and rich in linoleic acid. It is good for all kitchen purposes and, being quite thin, can be blended with thicker olive oil to advantage. Made into margarine spreads, it loses some of its health value, because it has to be hardened by hydrogenation, which turns some of the unsaturated oil into saturated. Sunflower oil is 68% unsaturated fat.

Corn oil A bland oil made from maize and lacking character. It is efficient for cooking, though it leaves a thick taste on the food. Although it can be used for salad dressings and vinaigrettes, it contributes no flavour of its own. Extremely high on the health ladder, being rich in linoleic acid, polyunsaturates (58%) and mono-unsaturates (29%).

Groundnut oil (peanut oil, in France *huile d'arachide*). A fine cooking oil, light and almost tasteless. It can be used in dressings with, or instead of, olive oil. High in linoleic acid and polyunsaturates.

Soya bean oil Although not commonly found on sale as such, it is usually the base of blended cooking oils. It is a particularly good, light, oil for cooking, and it's also high in linoleic acid and polyunsaturates (58%) and mono-unsaturates (25%).

Cottonseed oil Mostly used in food manufacturing for margarines, and canning fish. This oil is also high in polyunsaturates and linoleic acid.

Sesame seed oil Strong, nutty, toasted, aromatic character. Used as a seasoning in the Orient, especially by the Chinese, who splash a little on to a hot dish just before serving. Good source of linoleic and lecithin.

Walnut oil Prized for its flavour, added to strong-flavoured salads, such as beetroot, tomato and watercress. Rich in polyunsaturates. Expensive, but can be blended with a mild sunflower or groundnut oil. Doesn't keep well, so store in a dark place, or, better still, in the fridge.

Hazelnut oil Another speciality oil, delicious in dressings, and very healthy. Like walnut oil, does not keep well.

Coconut oil A heavy oil, which solidifies in its container like lard. Used in the tropics, where it's cheap, but is not recommended for the kitchen either gastronomically, or on health grounds, containing 91% saturated fat.

Palm oil Made from the nut of the oil palm, a solid, thick yellow paste, known as *dende* in Brazil where it gives many dishes a characteristic oily thickness. Similar to coconut oil, high in saturated fats (85%).

Ghee This is clarified butter, that is butter that has been boiled and strained of all the milk solids which cause it to burn when you fry with it. It keeps for months in a jar without refrigeration. You can clarify your own butter, heating it with water in a saucepan, then chilling in the fridge. When cold, remove the liquid and the scum of milk solids.

9

GUIDE TO THE LESS COMMON INGREDIENTS

Bacalao (Spain), *bacalhau* (Portugal) Dried salt cod. Hard with a very pungent smell, it has to be soaked for 4–6 hours in several changes of water to remove salt. Try to buy a thick piece.

Burghul, *bulgur* (in the Balkans), *pourgouri* (in Cypriot shops) Wheat which has been parboiled, then dried and cracked (in a mill) to various degrees of coarseness. Buy it from delicatessens, health-food shops and Cypriot stores.

Callaloo Thick, fleshy leaves of the *eddoe* or *taro* plant, a Caribbean root vegetable.

Chard, *Swiss chard* (or *blette*) Similar to, but firmer than spinach. The white stalk should be cooked separately.

Chinese five spices A mixture of aniseed, fennel, clove, cinnamon and sichuan (szechuan) pepper. Available in Chinese shops.

Chorizo (Spain), *chouriço* (Portugal) Hard sausage made with pork, garlic, paprika and other spices. Can be cooked or eaten raw.

Coriander Its green, strong-flavoured leaves give a distinctive flavour to Thai and Indonesian dishes. Also a key flavour in Mediterranean salads. Wrap in a plastic bag, fastened at the top, put in the salad compartment of the fridge, and it will keep for ages.

Doufu Chinese white bean curd. See tofu.

Feta cheese Salty, sour, low-fat curd cheese, from Greece and the Balkans.

Filo pastry Paper-thin sheets of pastry made from flour, water, vegetable oil and salt. Sold increasingly in supermarkets as well as in Greek food shops.

Haloumi A firm, white Greek cheese.

Labna Cream cheese made from yoghurt thickened by draining off the whey through thin muslin.

Lemongrass Lemon-flavoured grass stems, sliced into oriental dishes and soups.

Masa harina Special cornmeal flour used for making tortillas. The grains are slaked in lime-water before grinding, which gives a distinctive flavour.

Miso Paste made from fermented bean curd, high in protein and vitamins.

Okra (ladies' fingers) Green, pointed pod vegetable used to add interest to vegetable dishes in India and the Caribbean particularly.

Pancetta (Italy) Roll of fat belly of pork. Cured in salt and spices. Used as flavouring agent in sauces, fillings, vegetables and roasts.

Papaya Tropical fruit with oily content. Its acid juice softens pork or chicken by its enzyme activity.

Pecorino (Italy) Hard, ewes' milk cheese, similar in style to Parmesan, made with cows' milk. Pungent, salty taste, used for grating and cooking.

Pine nuts (pignoli) Kernels of the cones of the stone pine. Delicate, almond flavour. They are used in puddings and biscuits, and combined with basil in a pesto sauce for spaghetti.

Plantain Member of the banana family. Eaten both green and ripe (when the skin is black), but in both cases it must be cooked before it is eaten. It is served as an appetiser, in soups, as a starchy vegetable, or as a dessert. Sold in West Indian shops.

Sirene Balkan cheese, salty, dry, like feta.

Sweet potato Several varieties in white, pink, red, or purple. The flesh is white to yellow, firm, and sweet. Delicious baked and mashed.

Tahina Oily paste of ground sesame seeds bought in jars from Cypriot shops or wholefood stores.

Tocino (Spain), *toucinho* (Portugal) Salted pork fat. The nearest substitute is unsmoked speck from Hungary.

Tofu (doufu) Bean curd made from soya bean milk. It resembles soft, firm, white cheese and is sold in cake form. It is available fresh from oriental food shops and some wholefood shops.

Yam West Indian root vegetable, very starchy white flesh, pure in flavour.

GLOSSARY OF COUNTRIES AND RECIPES